Alfred Antoine Furman

Philip of Pokanoket

an Indian Drama

Alfred Antoine Furman

Philip of Pokanoket
an Indian Drama

ISBN/EAN: 9783743303768

Manufactured in Europe, USA, Canada, Australia, Japa

Cover: Foto ©ninafisch / pixelio.de

Manufactured and distributed by brebook publishing software (www.brebook.com)

Alfred Antoine Furman

Philip of Pokanoket

TO
UNITED STATES SENATOR
WATSON C. SQUIRE OF WASHINGTON,
IN TOKEN OF
THE MANY ACTS OF KINDNESS I HAVE RECEIVED FROM HIS HANDS,
THIS VOLUME
IS RESPECTFULLY INSCRIBED.

THE VOICELESS RACE.

The sun drops through that ancient roof of green
    Thatching your home not made by human hand,
    But nevermore on silent lake or land
    Shall what he viewed by him again be seen.
From the dark soil ye sprang and in that soil
    Have faded now, and no memorial left
    Save ruin, and a stern delight that kept
    Her throne in visioned minds when time a spoil
Had made of all things else. So let it be.
    Say, Gheezis breath was weary, and no more
    Blew summer in the branches of your tree.
Best is it that the wind from orient shore
    Should blast you, friendless hands tear down your name,
    And file a lien on your house of fame.

PHILIP OF POKANOKET.

PERSONS REPRESENTED.

POMETACOM, called PHILIP, *Chief of the Wampanoags.*
ANNAWAN, *Wampanoag.*
TATOSON, "
TUSPAQUIN, "
ALDERMAN, *Pocasset.*
AGAMAUG, "
TOTATOMET, *Seconet.*
SAMPONCUT, "
ANUMPASH, "
CANONCHET, *Narraganset.*
QUINNAPIN, "
POMHAM, "
UNCAS, *Mohegan.*
ONEKO, "
MONOKO, *Nipmuck.*
METACOMET, *Son of Philip.*
JOSIAH WINSLOW, *Governor of Plymouth.*
BENJAMIN CHURCH, *Commander of the Puritan Forces.*
CAPTAIN THOMAS LOTHROP.
CAPTAIN SAMUEL MOSELY.
CAPTAIN ROGER GOLDING.
WENONAH, *Squaw-Sachem of the Seconets.*
WOOTONEKANUSKE, *Wife to Philip.*
WANDA, *Wife to Samponcut.*
Indian Braves of the Allied Tribes, Squaws, Soldiers, Citizens.

SCENE : Dispersedly in Massachusetts and Rhode Island.

TIME : 1675–1676.

PHILIP OF POKANOKET.

ACT I.

SCENE I. POKANOKET. A spring at the foot of a cliff; above, under the trees, the lodges of the Wampanoags.

Enter ALDERMAN, *who bends to drink at the rock,* AGAMAUG *and* TATOSON.

   Agamaug.   Wah!
My brother's heart is sad.
   Tatoson. Can streams escaped from winter's hand
Mirror a sky of calm? These ears have drunk
A grievous tale.
   Agamaug.   Let the Wampanoag
Speak: open are the ears of Agamaug.
   Tatoson. Listen! In a deep glen where still at noon
Twilight binds up the face of day, I met
A runner who from Apaum lodges came,
Where, when his heart had withered and turned black,
Dwelt Sassamon.
   Alderman.   Have I not heard
The worms feed on him now?

Tatoson. Pocasset, his arms are long;
And after him they drag into the earth
Three of our braves.
   Agamaug. I am to learn.
   Alderman. Brother,
The whites, because he trod their moral ways,
Harbored his cause: and who shall hold their hand?
   Tatoson. Are the Pokanokets
Dogs to bear this? Can we say to the squaw
Wampapaquin, the Apaums have his scalp,
And in the pale-face field his nation fears
To reap revenge?
   Agamaug. Unhappily ye nursed
Hatred to Sassamon.
   Tatoson. 'Sh! A renegade,
The worship of his fathers' Manitou
Was not good in his eyes; but he would rub
His superstition's itch by bowing down
Before a thorn-crowned man, and in a book
Read how he died for him. Nathless, he coined
Falsehoods, and passed them in the white men's
     ears:
Our braves threw over him the net of death,
That snared them too.
   Alderman. Fancies thy Sachem that their act
Of friendship tastes?
   Tatoson. Pometacom
Travelled in month of leaves where the sun sleeps:
To hasten his return our fleetest brave
Unwinds his breath: Brothers, our young men live
In hovel of disgrace, if they shall lay
No axe at foot of this death-tree: in vain

This storm plant bears the blood of some slain chief
To paint our cheeks for war.
> [*Breaks off a blood-root poppy, and with its crimson juice smears his face and breast.*]

       Hist! here is the Chief
Coming with Annawan. Borrow with me,
While they confer, the shelter of a tree.
            [*Exeunt.*

   Enter PHILIP *and* ANNAWAN.

Philip.   Annawan,
I do not think a sweeter spring than this
Leaps to the sun; it travels through the earth
From house of purity, and brings us health.—
I would pass by a twenty rills though thirst
Shrivel my tongue, to quaff of thee.
> [*Takes a horn cup from his belt, fills it and drinks.*]

Annawan. By Wabun!
Philip. [*Passes rapidly to Annawan and whispers:*] I heard a twig
Snapped; there are moccasins: see what it is!
Annawan. [*Examines the foot-prints.*]
Wampanoag! May never pale-face come
Nearer than now!
Philip.   Ha! do they feel
The scalps burn on their heads?
Annawan. Nushkah! our eyes have been behind a cloud.
Sachem, their new-fledged purpose must not fly,
While we have breathing, into action's sky.
Philip.   Kah! A serpent by the fang
They take in me. How did they die?

Annawan.   As they had lived,
Strangers to fear.
　Philip.　I mean, by fire or steel: I know they went
Equipped with honor.
　Annawan.   Sachem, with me:
Hard by the palisades of Plymouth town
Looms up a gallows gaunt; and on its arms,
Rocked by the winds, bewept by pitying clouds,
The forms of Panoso and Mattashun
Swing to and fro; and flocks of sordid fowl
Fatten them at the crystal windows where
Looked out on this fierce world those candid souls.
A nobler end welcomed Wampapaquin:
For standing with his eyes unbound, his brow
Bared to the golden sun, erect, unmoved,
The message came written in leaden hail
Which sank him down drenched in more honest
　　　　blood—
Nushkah!—than musters in their arrogant veins
Since time began.
　Philip.   Their spirits pardon me!
Look down, ye braves, and register my vow.
In rank ye were the least among my tribe;
But here on ancient site of this your race
I swear your end deeply shall be avenged.
Wake, dogs of war! and with your ulcered tongues
Lick up the drops that so untimely flowed,
Till your swart veins shall swell to mountain size
And burst in pitiless havoc on the land.
With solemn hand married to your redress,
I now unbelt my hatred of the whites;
And bid it roam sleepless the bounds of earth
In quest of blood to sate its appetite.

Annawan.   Pometacom,
Justice shall come again on this wild scene,
And hallow thee.
   Philip.   Ay, Chief, if I should tell
What we have borne, meekly and humbly borne,
The tedious story must bankrupt the day,
And even be a debtor to the night.
   Annawan. Oh Sachem! shall words, and words alone,
Build up this flame?
   Philip.   No, Annawan,
The fuel of our wrongs shall feed the blaze
Till its red jaws devour their settlements.
Assemble here the warriors when the moon
Hangs on the western wall her silver bow.
Send wind-fleet messengers to Canonchet,
Bidding him to our war-dance lead his braves;
To the wile-loving Uncas and his chiefs
Whose fame on brow of deeds unspeakable
Redly is written; to the Pocasset Squaw;
To her who sways the ocean Seconets;
And all the tribes that moist with tears of rage
The scant meat eaten by grace of English hands:
White wampum to them send, of our resolve
A pledge, framed in fair words. Do not delay.
   Annawan.   This points to my desire.
I go, Pometacom.   [*Exit.*
   Philip.   I lean on thee!—
The arrow from the bow is sped. Hence, peace!
And crouch in slavish breasts: thou didst infect
Our valor's health with indolence and fear,
And played the pander to our virgin pride.
Come, painted war! and sack the house of life,

Hanging thy features with its ruby wealth,
Till they shall seem so noble in our eyes
That every forest child shall worship thee.

[Exit.

SCENE II.—SOGKONATE. A lodge on the seashore, with the Seconet village in the distance, amid tufts of coarse grass and clumps of dwarf pines.

ANUMPASH, *painting his face in the ocean mirror;* TOTATOMET, *in war dress and armed, pacing the sands.*

Totatomet. I loved her, Anumpash :
Not twenty whites with all their cloud of heart,
Dilated in the pure serene of love,
Could reach to mine. Our thoughts, our lives were twinned,
As buds to spring, as shadows to the night.
We sought all strange and solitary haunts—
The uncompanionable rock, the sea
In whose white mane I joyed to wind my hand,
And whirl away. For her I grappled death
What time a venomed brute crouched in the grass,
His fearful rattles shaking, lanced her side :
I sucked the wound, and of the poison drank
Deep draughts, to pension her with life. For her,
To signalize my prowess in her eyes,
I took the black bear in mine arms and fed
My hungry knife with his bold blood. And she
Would watch my coming with expectant eyes ;
And a warm glance rewarded all my toils.
Now all is changed ! And why ? Am I not held
The foremost warrior of the Seconets,
So far before in every woodland art

The foot of competition limps behind?
What maiden of the village would not bless
The happy hour that led her to my lodge?
That hell-sent pale-face hath bewitched the Squaw
With praises of her liquid eye, her hair
Falling adown her neck like midnight's wing:
His adder tongue hath charmed her silly wit,
And hissed away the favor she was wont
To rapture me. I hate him: he must die.
   Anumpash. Ay, let him die.
   Totatomet.   Hark, Anumpash!
The stalk of peace is rotten and decayed;
And weeds of strife grow in our quiet fields.
I offer her to bitter thoughts, and seek
War as a bride. The brave Wampanoags
Will hold a war-dance at Pokanoket,
And paint them for the fray, what time the moon
Her silver bow hangs on the western wall.
Haste we to gird our fortunes in their cause:
Some chance will point the way to my revenge.
   Anumpash. I am with thee.

Enter SAMPONCUT, *with nets on his shoulder.*

   Samponcut. Peace be with thee, Totatomet.
   Totatomet. We parted but this hour, and I am
      friend
Only to strife.
   Samponcut. What! hath an indigestion base
Usurped thy wonted humor's seat, and turned
The fur of thy serenity? In truth,
He is my mortal foe, and could I take
The varlet at advantage, I would trip
His heavy heels and pummel so his ribs,

He would shake off the arm of my acquaintance,
And never look me in the face again.
Whip him with a spare meal, the Meda says;
But I and fasting can no more agree
Than oil and water.

Totatomet. Ah! Samponcut,
The time hath indigestion, and it groans
To bear upon its back these slothful days.
Mix me in thine alembic what will cure
The jaundiced state, and I will fee thy skill
With boundless wealth of praise.

Samponcut. Oh, brave, what pay to hedge
Me from the winter winds! Yet for I love
Thy youth, I counsel thee. Thy mind is ill,
And host to vain desires. Content will splint
Thy broken hopes, heir thee to happiness.
Content hath a free hand: he scatters joys
On every step of this our mortal way.
Like the dull snail, he carries on his back
All that he owns; his patrimony is
The fair landscape; the ray of a June sun
His wampum all.

Totatomet. I understand
Nothing of this. Come, Anumpash!

Samponcut. Hold,
Totatomet! Wenonah hath forbid
Thy going hence. Afrenzied is thy mind
By fasting in the war-devoted grove;
Thou hast dressed up in battle garb; thy cheeks,
Thy massive breast with all the symbols dread
Painted, and shaven thy head till the scalp-lock
But now remains wherein the foe may twine
His dripping hand. To slaughter are thy thoughts

Neighbors, on trails of war will set thy feet.
No more to bask thee in the vivid sun
And nod the hours away ; no more to sit
Within thy wigwam's shade, and gloating pick
A partridge breast. In river of this past
Wade, and the voice of loss shall bid thee stay.
   Totatomet. I weep for thee, my mother Sogko-
      nate !
The rule deputed to a squaw whose cheek
Moulteth its ruby plume at voice of war :
Whose power is built on packs of foolish ones
Fettered to grossness. The six Pokanokets
Who came with offers from Pometacom
To seal a firm alliance of our tribes,
By pale-face wheedling and intrigue dismissed
With marks of outrage and contempt ; this hand
Disdained ; and in the chalice of my life
A brood of vipers dropped ! Oh ! that I had
The thunder's mouth to rattle in their ears
My loathing tongue !
   Samponcut.   Ho! ho! Totatomet,
Cannot our peaceful life roof in and close
Those towering thoughts which wander to the
      stars !
Thy totem bar this summer storm of Squaw
Wenonah thy best self curdle and cream:
Thy genuine merit will her coquetry
Outface, to thy devotion bow her choice.
But calm thy sea of passion ere it roll
Upon thy beach of fortune ; and beget
Pappooses none so choleric and rash.
   Totatomet.   Old man, I have no time, no wish,
To list these homilies. Within this bag

I have put up some acorns and parched maize;
And kindred spirits by the willows wait
Our coming, to join the heroes of the age.
Sunk in the ooze of sloth, crawl, Samponcut,
With belly groaning 'neath its load of food
Unto thine end: the feast of battle mine.
    Samponcut. But pray thee wait a moment while
        mine eyes
Feed on thy martial brow. In youth I heard
The dark tale of a warrior who like thee
Glory incensed; and if my strangered tongue
Trip not in memory's path, of him they said:
Lo! in his eye how stern command doth ride;
How swells his heart with passion's angry tide;
And in his legs there chafes a bridled steed
Shall chase the whites with more than mortal
    speed.
    Totatomet.   No lazy tide
Flows in thy throat! But moccasin of thine,
Catcher of eels, will never brush aside
The forest leaves, with braves on the war-path.
I pardon thee for that thy soul is mean,
And no time hath the face of battle seen.
Thy blood is stagnant, and it cannot feel
The perfect joy of war; what time we steal
With tomahawk uplifted on the foe,
Sprinkling the glad earth with his abject brain;
To dance with rapturous whoopings in the glow
Of burning houses; and to count our gain
Of guns and scalps and maidens pale with woe:
Then with wild pride fade in the woods again.
    Samponcut. No; I am fat and cannot run like
        thou.

Long hath our tribe hung round the neck of peace;
And I am only valiant 'gainst the waves
Whose pale-green shoulders nestle in the arms
Of these white sands. Rein in thy surly pride ;
And down life's stream with me serenely glide.
   Totatomet. When the bee drinks no more at honey-wells. [*Exit.*
   Anumpash. And the dew falls at noon. [*Exit.*
   Samponcut.   I breathe again!
A captive in the Mohawk towns he drank
Their spirit fierce. Dropped in these tranquil days,
He's like a goby jerked on the wan shore
With a bone hook. So shake my nerves again,
Brain fever puts me in a bed of leaves.
By Peboan! I doubt me if our shaved
Warriors glean profit in this field of war;
For fortune wears the pale-face in her heart,
And like a lover smiles on all his plans.
To let us sit beneath the tree of peace
Was wisdom in Wenonah, though her course
The white chief steered, who put to headlong rout
The gallants of our tribe, and stormed the fort
Of her affections. A moment of thy time,
Oh Manitou! thy servant pilfers now,
Beseeching thee to hold the Seconet
Nation pure of Wampanoags. I craved
Hard knocks on the head never, no, not I :
Though it is blamable—have the winds ears?—
Sweet braves, to say it in these iron times,
I own I love my life, and still prefer
To wade at ebb tide for a nest of clams
Than to adorn my lodge with long-haired scalps.

But now the golden scout of day is camped
Proudly upon the blue hills of the sky:
'Tis time that Wanda had prepared my meal—
Corn-cake, mussels, fat pemmican and teal.
Cherish thy stomach, braves, and all is well :
By that neglect our star of empire fell.   [*Exit.*

SCENE III.—POKANOKET. The centre of the Wampanoag village, a wide grassy space surrounded by the bark lodges of the tribe. On one side a huge fire of pine knots; on the other, a young oak stripped of its branches and planted in the earth as a war-pole. In a semicircle are seated, silent and grave, the leading chiefs, PHILIP, CANONCHET, UNCAS, TUSPAQUIN, ANNAWAN, POMHAM, while grouped by rock and tree the Sagamores and braves, ALDERMAN, AGAMAUG, ONEKO, QUINNAPIN, MONOKO, TATOSON, and others, Wampanoags, Narragansets, Pocassets, Nipmucks. Time : night, the new moon low in the western sky.

  Quinnapin. The trail of the Mohegans is long.
  Oneko. They see more glory on the brow of peace.
  Alderman. Say rather that the fiery blasts of war
Shrivel their leaves of courage up.
  Quinnapin. A pattern here ! Wenonah's braves
Skulk in their lodges.
  Monoko.   Yet would they scorn to prowl
In lodges of their friends.
  Quinnapin.   Ha !
  Oneko.   And is it true

Ye bartered all? Not even a poor ditch
To fight them in!
  Quinnapin.   An thou wilt fight,
The rabbit wears a valiant heart and cries
'Esa' to the she-bear.
  Oneko.   Nay, drinker of fire!
In fields of war my victories are won,
Not reaped in arms of squaws.
  Quinnapin.   Oh Unktahee!
No scalp thy belt dangles but it was gleaned
In head of some decrepit wretch who blessed
The Master of Life thou kindly didst snuff out
The candle of his woes. Yerks forth thy hand
Some wintry hairs, straightway thy fawning
      tongue
Whispers, Lo! here a brave. Woman!
  Oneko.   Thy soul, if thou hast one,
Howlings inherit! If my lodge were bare
As thine of noble trophies, I would beg
The first pappoose make in my lily heart
Bed for his knife of lath. Dog!
  Tatoson.   Sheath your disputes! To-morrow
      you shall drink
Your fill of blood.
  Quinnapin.   Go to! Next he eats salt
Like any white.

      Enter TOTATOMET *and Seconet braves.*

  Tatoson.   The paint of the Seconets!
  Totatomet.   You called for fighting men,
And we are here.
  Warriors.   Ugh! ugh! ugh!

Philip. [*Arises and advances to the war-post.*]
                    My worthy Seconets!
You rock my hopes in cradle of success.—
Mohegan, thou art welcome : on thy head
The years sit lightly ; thy great voice of fame
Our every wigwam hears.—Canonchet, here
Be free! The heritage of a proud name
Never did fall in purer hands ; subdued
Our honors stand before the face of thine.—
Brothers, you tread on your own soil.
    Canonchet.   Our hearts are glad, Pometacom.
    Uncas. Sachem, mine eyes are bleared ; they
            cannot see
The calumet of peace.
    Philip.   No sacred smoke,
Uncas, will curl thee from that bowl to-day.—
Brothers, your ears have heard
The cry that rises from Pokanoket ;
You were not sleeping when our arrows came
Covered with blood. What then? A fifty years
Have fallen from the wrinkled hand of time
Since first the pale-face seized these virgin shores,
And sowed such changes in our field of fate.
They were but few ; and on Patuxet rock
Huddled, their hosts were gloomy rain and cold
That chain the spirited blood in cells of death ;
And hunger, shearing off life's golden fleece.
My father, Massasoit, hand in hand
Travelled with gentleness ; and to his breast,
In luckless day, he took the frozen viper
And warmed it into life. He gave them corn ;
And counsel from his hospitable mind ;

And built them lodges in the red man's land.
His kindness was the author of our fall:
Quenched at its birth this fatal brand of strife
Had sputtered out in ashes of his power,
And we had held our fathers' heritage.
They waxed in greatness like the moon : at first
A silver thread lacing the waist of heaven,
It grows a ball of brightness till its orb
In beauty lights the ebon cheek of night.
Over the barren seas their sail-winged barks
Hundreds of white men bore. Their towns arose
Like spirits of the dark, with motion fringed
The curving bays, the rapid rivers' banks,
Whose solitude had echoed but the cries
Of red men since the earth was young. Like mist
We melted in the rays of this new sun.
Our lands are coaxed to flow, despite our will,
Into their hands; our hunting grounds, dark, pure,
Betrayed to light; our warriors from their faith,
None nobler now, seduced, and taught to pray
To unknown gods, the Spirit who rides in storms,
Who loved our fathers and our fathers loved,
Torn from the sky! We quaffed the crystal spring,
And reason kept him on his noble throne:
Now in the burning waves of their new drink
Founders the vessel of our native pride.
Their laws invade our immemorial rights
Bequeathed from sire to son, and snare our feet
Walking in the old ways; and lo! our braves
Death-doomed without a trial by their peers,
The gallows arbitrating! Ye forest sons!
Lords of yourselves and born to liberty,
Whose merits should stand free and unabashed

Before the eye of fortune, will ye lick,
Fallen so low, the hand of this harsh change,
And perish in the furious tide of wrong?
Or shaking off your dream of apathy,
Free our beloved Kinshon from the yoke?
Brothers, decide! Pometacom hath spoke.
             [*A long silence.*

   Uncas. [*Arises in his place and bends slightly
             forward with raised-up hand.*]
   I seem to hear the voice of other days
Buried in silence; music that will charm
Trees and dull rocks out of their patient forms
To follow thee admiring. But are thy braves
Rebels to life, that they will take up arms
Against the hand of fate? Is the Great Spirit
Recruiting his bright legions in the sky,
And drafts Wampanoags? Pometacom,
What gifts hast thou from nature: use them well!
Let not ambition leap upon thy will,
To drive thee in the bitter gulf of war
Scattered with bleaching hopes. Sit in thy lodge,
And let thy lusty braves the unfooted wilds
Wander by side of peace.
   Pomham.   Sachem, who can divorce
The red man from his bride of war? Her form
Beckoned his eye in lone antiquity,
And taught his arm the practice of revenge.
In paths of lowness let Mohegans tread:
The Narraganset bosom cannot nurse
Children of fear. The finger of the whites
Hath smeared a dark spot on the red man's lodge,
And only blood can wash it out.

Uncas.   I deem in house of age
Prudence should dwell. Alas! my words are cold.
The sceptre of the Sachem's eloquence
Waving your fervid souls to battle's edge,
I do not sway: the plummet of my thoughts
I can but drop in wisdom's pure, cold well.
The lurid face of war with serpents twined,
I worshipped: ere your hands could stretch the
    bow,
Down from his gloomy brow had I plucked fame,
And gorged the ashen fruits of victory
Purchased by streams of blood. But is it good
To press our lips unto a burning stream?
To so dire wharf mooring our nation's bark?
Where is the Pequod race whose genius supped
From the red hand of war? In the great Eye
That overlooks the world and reads our lives,
Ye are rebuked if their so fiery fate
Scorch not the lustre of your new design.
From them I draw my blood; and when they stood,
The forest lords, mantled in bright renown,
Around the war-post could a thousand braves
Rally, the song obsequious to death
In frenzy chanting, frenzy and despair.
In evil hour they stirred the English power
Sleeping till then; and like a drought-lit fire
With crimson feet raging in autumn woods,
It fell on them consuming. Where are they now?
The earth can tell: like seared and yellow leaves
Chased by the wind and crammed in winter's maw,
Their blighted honors strew the ground of time.
Softly doth age my knot of life untie;
Soon must I step down in the mortal stream,

And taste the inevitable wave of death :
Yet not so dim mine eyes but they can see
Yawning a grave for them who string their hopes
On pale-face conquest.   Ye stumblers, I have said.
   Monoko.   I rub the cheek of Uncas, and I see
A pale-face skin : the whites have given him
A petticoat, and in his lodge with squaws
Have bid him stay.   Soonever he hears move
His masters' lips, come, he comes ; go, he goes ;
And eats the crumbs that from their tables fall.
But in the foretime when the noble sun
Climbed out the crimson windows of the east,
Until he laved his brow in western waves,
He saw no slave.   Sachems, I am too old
To learn the lessons of obedience ;
And I had rather go into the earth
While freedom lives, than bear her to the tomb.
   Alderman.   Ay, Monoko, it flies on wing of truth :
If Pequods tread no more the provident earth
Uncas can tell : were not his arrows aimed
At Pequod hearts?   A red man's memory
Is longer than the justice of the whites.
   Annawan.   Braves, your proud words
Roll up the shadows from my memory's sky.
Methinks I see that oak so serious clad
In rustling robe of green, and lifting high
A storm-swept head above its forest kin,
Felled in the morning of renown.   But yet
From out its prostrate fertile trunk shall spring
A well-starred tribe whose roots shall pierce the
      earth
Still deeper, and whose brow shall kiss the skies.
Why should our courage faint beneath the breath

Of Yengeese fortune? Every thought of peace
Disown while breathe our air and tread our soil
They who should dwell in flaming heart of hell.
   Totatomet.   Wampanoag,
No Seconet but thou hast fathered me.
My thought is naked as the common air,
And leaps to press the lips of thine intent,
In its own strength reposing, and your right:
For me one hour of sloth-reproving strife
Outweighs a century of sluggish life.
   Tuspaquin.   ' I learn the way!
Give all the braves to know that purer blood
Than mountain dew, on which thy heart hath fed!
The springs may dry, if yet to slake our thirst
Veins of the pale-face flow.
   Quinnapin. Brothers, is Apaum fortune built so
      strong,
The Narraganset arm may not reach up
And tear it down? Lead on, Pometacom,
And death shall own allegiance to this arm.
   Warriors.   Ugh! ugh! ugh!
   Canonchet.   Pometacom,
I pledge mine arms and Narraganset bands
To clothe in acts thy purpose and commands.
   Uncas. Great Narraganset, kindle not a fire
In whose red arms thy nation will expire.
   Pomham. He counsels thee whose father he
      betrayed.
   Canonchet. Not that way, Shawomet! The hand
      of time
Hath healed that wound: the dead are happier far
Than base ones breathing.—But ye, alone as now,
Can ye find honor in your enslaved lodge

Paled round with curses deep; and be content
To barter skins for scarlet coats and guns;
To search the wrinkled shore for purple shells,
And drill you strings of wampum—trade of
    squaws?
Can ye with clean hands to the Great Spirit's
    lodge
Carry your lives? Fawn on the pale-face hand,
Hearts treason-bit, and fix your perilled eye
On Plymouth lips so dear. My soul is free:
The air of peace blows like a furnace blast,
And stifles it.—
Dig up the hatchet buried now too long,
And glad me with your ancient battle song.
Lo! here I strike.

[*Advances to the war-post and buries his hatchet in it. Rude drums. The* WAMPANOAGS *advance and chant their war-cry.*]

THE WAR-SONG.

I.

' The chain of peace is snapped in twain,
  Our sturdiest braves in ambush slain;
    But squaws alone will weep:
  Be ours to grasp the tomahawk,
  And through the files of battle stalk
    To bathe in vengeance deep.

    Ye forest sons! arise! arise!
    And ring your war-whoops to the skies;
    And where a foe shall rear his head
    Bequeath him to the silent dead.

2.

Your fathers' wrongs call from the earth;
Your own chase from your breast its mirth,
    For vengeance crying loud:
No longer creep from birth to death;
But rise and fling away your breath
    In voice of triumph proud.

3.

See from its grave the hatchet leap,
In blood the face of foes to steep,
    While round the warriors smile:
He who shall die in cause like this,
Shall wash his soul in tides of bliss
    On Manitou's blue isle.

Agamaug. Would this were heart of all our enemies! [*Strikes.*
Tatoson. No way but this:
    A warrior's life is bliss. [*Strikes.*
Uncas. Their minds turn out of doors the one wise voice.
Master of Life! if still with favor on thy red
Children thou lookest, hang not on their hopes
This insane veil that blinds and muffles up
The face of reason. Come! We may not stay:
Their feet are wending on a tragic way.—
We go, Pometacom; but come what may,
My wonder holds thee more than common clay.
    Oneko. [*To* QUINNAPIN.] I see a halter dangling in the air,
To clasp thy gullet in its fingers bare.

Quinnapin.   I see a whip suspended in the air,
Which I would clutch to welt thy shoulders bare ;
But I disdain to soil me with such fry,
When noble souls await my hand to die.
   Oneko.   Perchance the future may reserve for me,
That I may lay it, Quinnapin, on thee.
                              [*Exeunt* UNCAS *and* ONEKO.
   Philip.   Thy years be honored !—
And yet we should have known a generous thought
Poured never from his lips.   But it is well.
My braves are numerous as the sparkling sands
On which the ocean clasps his emerald hands ;
Their hearts are panting for the battle fray :
I could not if I wished it say them nay.   [*Strikes.*
[*All the chiefs and warriors in succession advance to the war-pole and hack it with their hatchets ; then they pass around it in a circle and chant the burden of a battle song :*
            We will tread on the heads of the foe,
            In the arms of the dust lay them low.
At the conclusion they turn to PHILIP *and salute him with tumultuous and joyful cries.*]
   Philip.   Sachems, warriors, Narragansets, tribes-
               men,
And all bound with me in this belt of war,
Falters my tongue on mountain of your worth
Too high for my weak praise to overclimb.
A presage this of triumph and renown,
If constancy shall even-footed run
With valor's steps, and each on honor wait.
Let no division in your counsels steal,
The rock on which the Pequod cause was wrecked,

And I from victory to victory
A path will blaze ; jewel your hands with spoil
That shall outmint the coinage of your dreams ;
And weigh your belts with scalps down to the
    ground ;
And choke your wigwams' mouth with captive foes;
And build your memory a house of fame
To dwell forever in.
   Warriors.   Ugh ! ugh ! ugh !
   Canonchet.   Pometacom,
We walk the clouds with thee.
   Philip.   The rich reality shall beggar it.
Now to your lodges till to-morrow's sun
Over Pocasset peering see our work begun.
                                        [*Exeunt.*

SCENE IV. SOGKONATE. The Seconet village. Before the lodge of WENONAH on the seashore. Moonlight.

      Enter WENONAH *and* CHURCH.

   Wenonah.   Besides, white chief,
A bitter discontent strides through the tribe,
Chiding my action with a saucy tongue :
The head of the revolt, Totatomet,
Whose gloomy spirit nursed in battle's arms,
Demanded that the wind of Sogkonate,
Freighted with war, should blow in Philip's sails.
   Church. Wenonah, in this cause thou hast invited
Reproach, danger perhaps : thy deed outruns
My swiftest tongue of praise.
   Wenonah.   It is not that, pale-face ;
For thee I would do that would swallow up

All other doing ; but I am but weak.
In voice of eloquence and fame of deeds
That pour a glory on the raging blood,
Resides a chieftain's power : commands are smoke
Which, saddled on the air, flees into space,
When linked to no deserving.
 Church.   My people's debt,
And thine own worth, the best blood of my heart
Forever seals to thee.
 Wenonah.   Pale-face, believe
'Twas a slight token of my authentic heart,
Liegeless till now, to throw my feeble will
Across the track of their desires. When time
Shall lead a new occasion to my door,
With truer welcome will I take its hand.
 Church. Thou art made up, compact and firm,
Of all true qualities.
 Wenonah. If thou say so,
And censures all the world, I walk in joy.
 Church. Wenonah, doubt me not.
 Wenonah.   It seems a dream
Whose veil the morning's hand will tear away,
And with the morning flee.
 Church.   On such a night
Never let day-star rise !
 Wenonah. Oh pale-face, standing here in solemn rays
Of night's great lamp, with spirits of my dead
Hovering around to witness thy fond words,
Tell me, can love's weak hand clasp on thy life
But so the fetters of a red dominion ?
Haply it is some fancy that will die
When the pinched snows of absence fall on it ;

Some passion, surfeited by futile charms,
Drowsy shall grow in afternoon of joy;
And I would find naught in the weary world
To succor me despairing.
 Church.   Wenonah, wean
That offspring of thine obdurate doubts: if I
Unworthy prove, thrust in thy young men's hands
The ruthless steel to loot and ransack all
My treasury of life; let young love be
By such relapsing slain, and the old hate
Beleaguer man's false heart.
 Wenonah.   Forgive me, Church;
'Twas only love that counselled me to doubt.
In marriage many chiefs have sought my hand:
Gifts to my lodge their braves have brought to buy
Consent to their proposals: they have come
Themselves in feathered dress that domineers
The eye, to seat them silent by my side,
Pleading with looks and sighs their amorous cause.
In all of them the tongue of some defect
Wrangled with their proud state, and silenced it
In my imagination. When my eye
Wandered to thee, its high unlorded glance
Was taken prisoner by thy noble mien;
While reason sat subdued by the great fame
Of strength and skill thou bearest in the world.
I would wed such a man; or I would live
Queen of myself, reigning in solitude.
 Church.   I wear no more,
Wenonah, on my life the bloom of youth;
And till this time I was content to be
A dallier with love; to tread the earth

Alone, leading my passions to the tomb;
But now my ways are consecrate to thine.
   Wenonah. Alas! the time poisons my brood of
      hope.
Thy people call thine arm to their defence,
And duty's stern hand girds thee for the strife.
Thy sword will smear its silver lips with blood
Housed in my nation's veins, and hatred deep
Will fix a gulf between thy race and mine:
For every fear my mind a refuge is!
   Church. Wenonah dear, let not those cares
Creep on thy cheek, nor livid thoughts of war
Usurp the peaceful musings of thy life:
Thy nation will not sail its crimson waves,
But lie in port of peace. When it is past,
My fortune in this island will I cast;
Building a wigwam in the wilderness
Where love and thou the solitude shall bless.
   Wenonah.   This is the trance,
The vision of my life! That I could clip
The pinions of old Time, so he should sit
All-patient at our feet, this quietude
Stretching to crack of doom! Why wilt thou go?
   Church. Wild-flower, gathered in desert of my
      life!
I will return on wings of swift desire,
To bathe my longing looks in thy deep eyes,
What time my duty I discharge to make
Report at Plymouth town: anxious they wait
Tidings how this disease infects the land;
And if the Seconets, in peace delighting,
With friendship's hooks are grappled to them still,
While other tribes flow in the sea of war.

But where I go, whatever fate I see,
In my fond heart thou liv'st eternally.
 Wenonah. Ah me! too early found, or found too
  late!
Would we were anchored in the days of peace!
This love fixes a stigma on my creed
Which should, I know, by every forest rule
Counsel to fortitude. The haggard wilds
Peopled with grim Pokanokets will rise
Ever before me, and their shadows stern
Invade on foot of dream the realm of sleep.
Oh! leave me pattern of that absolute heart
That feeds thy courage with its iron blood,
So I may face the future with a brow
Laden with smiles, and be serene as thou.
 Church. Dear one, dearer than ever now!
The forest is a glass where we may see
The imperturbable God and learn His ways;
And while a ruby hand knocks at the heart,
Fingers of hope should open it. Again
I lay my parting on thy cheek and say,
Farewell.
 Wenonah. I cannot teach my tongue that word:
It locks my lips with dumbness. I could burn
In the fierce flames of my relentless hate
Those rebel syllables, that they no more
Pillage my peace.
 Church. Sweet Seconet, thy will
Is sovereign here; mine can but humbly page
The heels of thy desire. But see! the dawn
With amber feet is pacing up the east,
And calls me laggard.
 Wenonah. No, 'tis not the dawn,

But some belated meteor in his flight
To trysting-place beneath the canopy
Of purple gloom, with yon enraptured star
Whose sapphire eyes beckon him gladly on.
 Church. To thee, my queen, I swear the night is young;
Those jealous streaks that hem the dress of day,
But keener glances of night's sentinels
Stretching their fiery necks to view on earth
A perfect love. Be this my throne!
 Wenonah.   Never usurper fear!
 Church.   First fall the heavens!
Weapons, lie there! or rather house your forms
Deep in these sands; for I subaltern am
Only to love.
         [*Throws down his arms.*
 Wenonah. A rarer strain is this
Than the west wind for my tribe's Manitou,
Harvests and puts away.
 Church.   Never till now
When beauty came in state, would my heart bow.
 Wenonah. That happies me yet more, and pales the light
Of all my fondest hopes: yet thou must go.
 Church. Be firm! Turned is the tide, and the lithe waves
Fawn at our feet; so shall misfortune, too.
 Wenonah.   Before I had not lived: if now—
 Church.   Nay, clothed in this delight
I am to paltry checks of mortal arm
Intrenchant as the air.
 Wenonah.   The village stirs; the night
Faints at the foot of day. In thine own hands!
         [*Picks up his arms.*

Church. My mission was forgot.
Wenonah. I have ensnared
Thy resolution in the net of my fond words,
And made thy will a by-word and naught else
But mockery. Pardon my sin.
Church. Oh! such sweet sin
Would tempt the angels from their banks of light
To harp their songs to thee.
Wenonah. I think they have let down
A mansion of delight where only bliss
Is servitor to me. But touches it
The thought that thou must go, it vanishes
And all is dark again.
Church. The scowling face of duty I will push
Back in his cave—
Wenonah. No! linger thou must not
Till the next wave foams on the shore. Away!
Over night's hills fast climbs the morning gray.
Church. Alas! that it should be intruding day!
I go, Wenonah, but in thought I stay.
[*Exit. Wenonah sinks in the door of the lodge.*

ACT II.

SCENE I.—PLYMOUTH. A room in Governor Winslow's house. The walls covered with forest trophies; in the centre of room a long table littered with letters, books, and maps.

WINSLOW, LOTHROP, *and* MOSELY, *seated.*

Winslow. [*Rising.*] Such is the child
Of our diplomacy! We bent on them
The gracious smiling face, soothing their pride
With gifts their rudeness loved. Our sacred book
We sent into their huts, haply it might
File down their spirits rough to deeds of peace,
And knit our lives in amity's soft bands.
When strong necessity hath ruled the hour
Our weakness showed a visage masked in frowns,
Their perfidy rebuking; while our heart
Trembled at face of its temerity.
Nor have we feared to plunge the battle's gage
Down at their feet, and risk the worst of fate,
Though but a fringe on their great cloth of war,
Rather than meekly yield to insolent threats
That would uncrown our prestige in their eyes,
And send our mastery to wander in contempt.
But all in vain! This Philip's restless soul
No threats may cower, no kindness may cajole:
As darkness ever hangs on edge of light,

So on our frontiers hang his imps of night
Portending ruin.—Who knocks?

     Enter CHURCH.

    Our worthy scout! Welcome!
Church.   Would I bore news
Were welcome too!
 Winslow. Travel-stained thou art—thy face
Shadows the vale of woe.
 Church.   Dear Governor,
Prepare thy mind for ill.
 Winslow. I feel what thou wouldst say :
Peace droops her gentle head, for wolfish war
His reddened fangs hath buried in her breast.
But where hath Philip struck?
 Church.   At Metapoiset eight are dead ;
And on the altars of their naked forms
Cruel indignities the fiends have heaped :
Their gashed and mangled bodies cast a damp
Upon the dazed beholders—gory heads
Stuck up on poles, glare fixed and stony eyes
Mocking revenge dealt out to them who slew
The convert Sassamon.
 Winslow. Oh, piteous sight!
 Lothrop. Cunning Philip! His patient craft
Mousing pretexts to kindle war, pounced on
That shadow of an injury to weave
The jealous tribes in union, who till now
Put on no strong desire to plunge them in
His wild ambition's stream. Them we must teach!
 Mosely. Captain, doth not this rising run
Before the steps of Philip's plot? I hear
Mount Hope Wampanoags of corn in ground

A thousand acres have, which policy
Before the march of war would never plant
For fire to reap.
 Church. Mosely, perchance our fears to hood-
  wink ; yet
The Sachem's wiles or his credulity
Recoiled from striking the initial blow :
A whimsical opinion in their minds
Dwells, victory's face at last would frown on them
Who first shed blood. Therefore his orders ran,
Plunder the Swanzey farms outlying ; maim,
Drive to the woods, the cattle and the sheep,
But not unless chided by bloody means
Reply in tongue of death. A quarrel rose
With a Pokanoket reeling in drink,
And one into whose home he flung the flames :
The savage bit the dust. Then all restraint
Despair unleashed : the painted braves with hate
Swollen, deeply their keen blood-hunger sate.
 Mosely. What tribes hath Philip welded to his
  cause ?
 Church. The Narragansets do espouse his war,
Who bring a thousand warriors in the field :
If good success shall perch on his first stroke
The Nipmucks, Abenakis, and the hordes
Peopling the shaggy forests of the north,
Cement it with their strength.
 Winslow. Forsake us not, be captain to us, God !
Doomed are the settlements if thou thy face
Avert, nor lead us with thy stretched-out hand !
 Mosely.   Do none of all the tribes
Turn here a friendly face, or sit them down
In wigwam of neutrality ?

Church. The Seconets, who count four hundred
    braves,
Would not baptize this fearful child of war
With their alliance; the Mohegan chiefs
Present at the war-dance, refused to grasp
The hand of the rebellion, but withdrew,
The plotted war condemning.

    Enter ONEKO *and Mohegan braves.*

Winslow.   Neither by knock
Announced, nor message, enter you!
    Church.   It is the forest mode.
    Oneko. Our father will forgive us, since we come
Holding the branch of peace.
    Winslow.   Mohegan then?
    Oneko.   Oneko is my name; and when I call
Uncas my father, drink your ears a name
With greatness goes.
    Winslow.   Honored it is, on our regard
Grafted by many friendly acts.
    Oneko.   Apaum, open thine ears:
The anger of Pometacom is kindled
Against his pale-face brothers; it hath raised
Tempests of war to desolate your towns:
His braves will travel in that blood-soaked path,
But Uncas and his children will not light
The dread fire; the chain of friendship they will
    keep
Bright and unbroken.
    Winslow.   We hold thee, Sagamore,
In close affinity: gifts shalt thou bear
To the great Chief whose many-wintered head
With fame is bound, in token of our love.

But them who have awoke this sad contest,
Such punishment awaits, and overthrow,
Nothing more dire their Mitchi-Manitou
Condemns below. And now our runners we will send
To warn the colonists the die is cast,
And misery plans a foray in the ranks
Of their calm life. Thou, versed in Indian wiles,
                              [*To* Church]
Shalt take a company of Bradford's men,
And with our veteran Mosely who hath seen
War's face under Jamaica's eye of fire,
Co-operate as the occasion's hand
To best results may point.—Lothrop, thy years
Are in their April leaf ; and hence I charge
That thou on Church his long experience lean,
And be a pupil in his forest art.
Disputes about seniority of rank
Must bow to the young peril of the hour
Perchance shall blink the bold eye of your worth:
The common weal relies on you.
  Church. Governor, in the fierce school of Indian arts
A little I have learned : that little I
Freely do offer to the colony's use.
  Winslow. Thy modesty is equal to thy worth.—
My friends, prepare to march at morrow's dawn.
The Lord will be our shield, and great reward ;
Our rock and our defence ; a cloud by day,
A pillar of fire by night.—Braves, of your plans
Something our enterprise would taste.
                              [*Exeunt.*

SCENE II.—THE CONNECTICUT VALLEY. A forest of oaks and yellow pines crossed by an Indian trail.

PHILIP *standing motionless beside a tree. Enter* ANNAWAN *on stealthy foot, examining the ground.*

Philip. Is the trap set?
Annawan. Ready to spring.

Enter TOTATOMET.

Philip. This is our eye.—Thy haste is eloquent:
They come this way?
Totatomet. See!
  [*He walks along like a tired person.*
      The September sun
Too fondly kisses them : the wagons groan
Under heaps of red corn and new-made arms :
Sleeps discipline.
Philip. How many?
Totatomet. [*Moves his hand rapidly around his head.*] For each belt two.
Philip. How far?
Totatomet. Pometacom, the distance have I run
While drifted yonder cloud across the sun.
  Philip. Our genius lays its fatal hands on them!
A slender stream crosses the road below :
Annawan, let twenty of thy best braves
So post them that their aim command the ford :
Myself will lead the onset on the flanks.
The debt I owe thee, Seconet, will pay
Our spoils of triumph in the coming fray.
Away! and watchful of the signal be :
We'll drink again the wine of victory.
                              [*Exeunt.*

SCENE III.—THE SAME. A road crossing a stream
bordered with rocks.

Enter CHURCH, *emerging from the forest.*

Church. At last!
If calculation in the scale of truth
Were weighed, here should I meet the Hadley men;
But the slack oxen and the staggering heat
Their movements tie to slowness. I am warned
By silent tongues to dread this expedition;
For more than once I stumbled on the trail
Of prowling redskins, and I make no doubt
War parties lurk them in these very woods.
Lothrop is rash, and hath a heady will
No hand of caution in a leash can hold :
His Sugarloaf success unbonneted his pride
So that it leaps at face of higher fortune.
What's that? The tramp of feet and wagons' roll.
Startle the drowsy air. I'll reconnoitre. [*Exit.*

Enter LOTHROP *at head of troops, and* CHURCH, *meeting.*

Church. Good-morrow, Captain.
Lothrop. Well met, my hardy forester.
I deemed thee many leagues away : what chance
Conducts thee here?
Church. No chance but intent leads my steps.
Apprised of thy design, a band of braves
At night the river crossed, and by a march
Rapid, are posted in thy van.
Lothrop. Well, let them come.
Church. What dost thou say?
Lothrop. I fear them not.
Church. Consider this :

Thy force is weak, unable to contend
With the great arm of danger in thy path.
Scouts I despatched to warn thee of the risk ;
But they at Philip's hands have met their fate.
Leaving with Mosely my command, I came
Unheralded, to urge thee halt thy troops :
By marches forced our veteran bands advance,
And union is forerunner of success.
    Lothrop.   Church,
Thy trouble pays thee merely for thy pains.
It is not like thy valor's lips will press,
In this dull march, the bloody cheek of war.
No Indian skulking in the silent aisles
Of pine and oak, no trail of their swift feet,
Have we descried since Deerfield from our sight
In distance faded : Philip, victory-flushed,
Under the larches of his native swamps
Reposes, satisfied.
    Church.   Pshaw!
Thou art a 'prentice in his trade of war.
I can set in thine eyes a commonplace
Shall be the jailer of thy confidence.
Seest thou this wintergreen with red cheek crushed,
Sprawled on the ground ? Upon the hectic leaves
That intoed print, proclaiming in this hour
Red men have passed ? I would not buy your lives
At a pin's worth when sets to-morrow's sun.
Philip is like the vagrant wind : to-day
Fast sleeping in the chambers of the south,
The path of air unwounded by its tread ;
To-morrow, a dark spirit from the north
With lightning helmeted, and at his back
Battalions of wild storm.

Lothrop.   Enough!
Fears from the purse of fancy, vain alarms,
I borrow not.
    Church.   So they at Wikabaug,
Proud in their strength and thralls of confidence,
Unqualitied, have in a bondage gone
No price can ransom back.
    Lothrop.   No more! Hang on my name
A merited contempt if I retreat.
    Church.   Better a wise retreat than overthrow.
    Lothrop.   Wilt thou have done?
    Church.   My God!
Preserve at least a common vigilance.
Never a scout thrown out to guard thy flanks;
Nor frowns at this disorder in the ranks
An eye of discipline: precautions are
Breast-plates to war, and half the victory win.
Trust my experience; for to him whose ways
Are kin to redskin wiles this silence waves
Signals of danger. Rather I believe
Each tree will ope its brown and furrowed breast
To thrust on our rapt gaze a host of foes,
Than we in safety stand.
    Lothrop.   Well, thou hast said:
Doubtless thy fear is parent to thy thought.
    Church. No, boy, I never knew the name of fear:
Its foot hath crossed the threshold of men's hearts,
But never walked in mine. Self-satisfied,
Live in the old darkness, and on thy morn
Never a truth-star rise!
    Lothrop.   I know thee, Church.
It is thine aim to gather in thy hands
All power: no victories must be won save those

Sanctioned by thee. I have the Essex men,
The flower of valor, none of them ashamed
To speak unto the enemy in the gate:
Defeat will flee before them. On! on!
                      [*The march resumed.*

         Enter a Soldier, hastily.

How now! Thy face is white as any ghost's
That roams through graves by night. What! dumb
   as death?
         Enter a second Soldier.
Canst *thou* speak?
[*Yells arise on all sides accompanied by showers of arrows and reports of guns.*]

   Second Soldier. The event outstrips my tongue.
   Church.   An ambuscade! Take to the trees!
   Lothrop. I am struck. Oh, thou mine of wisdom
      rare!
This had not come if I had delved me there.
                    [*Exeunt in confusion.*

[*War whoops and shouts. Enter, fighting, whites and Indians; then* CHURCH *pursued by* TOTATOMET.]

   Totatomet. Surrender, pale-face! or thy life is
      bond
Unto the next stroke of my tomahawk.
   Church. Villain, away! I do not hold my life
Subject to any arm on earth.
   Totatomet.   White chief, no nimble heels
May save thee, but my friendly wishes can.

Church. In this good arm alone!
Totatomet. Look round thee! See on every hand
The bodies of thy comrades choke the land
With blood. Mine arms are drunk with it. Thy death
Will not put in thy cause a single breath.
Church. He talks to me as one who values life
Begged from a foe in stress of mortal strife.
Take from my path thy damned form!
Totatomet. Why not thou?—
I would tear out his flesh at the red stake
Shred by shred.—Pale-face, the rose of Sogkonate
Will wither at thy fall.
Church. Thou demi-devil!
Dost thou think I will spend a word to buy
Ages of captive breath? Make way! These slain
Nerve me with their mute eloquence.
Totatomet. Through walls of foes
Thy path to freedom lies.
[*They continue to fight.*
Enter PHILIP, ANNAWAN, *and braves.*

Philip. Who is it here dares live when we have set
Death on his throne?
[*Strikes down* CHURCH'S *arm, and the others secure him.*]
The pale-face Chief! A prize worth all the rest!
Now guard him well. Smothered with victims is
The mouth of death: reserve him for the stake.
Totatomet. A prize, Pometacom, a prize!
My hatred for his cup of torture cries.
Philip. The pale-face pays my debt: the Chief is thine.—

My braves, come round me; let me see the joy
That rides in your wild eyes, and through the paint
On your high cheeks peeps forth in solemn smiles.
This is the sovereign moment of your days,
That crowns your acts with brass-enduring bays.
Like the tornado launched from depths of space,
Your bolts have fallen on this evil race;
And everywhere your glorious steps have trod
The pale-face clasps in death the crimson sod.
Already panic to their towns is fled;
And if at night "Wampanoag" be said,
The hearts of bearded men knock at their side,
As if the current of their veins were dried
In the fierce sun of your immortal hate,
And they that instant felt the stroke of fate.
Now feast ye on the store of corn and wine
This victory gives; and to the sun divine
Where dwells the Manitou in lodge of fire,
Lift up your shouts for the confusion dire
He hurls upon your enemies. The slain
Shall fringe your belts with deeply valued gain
Of scalps. What ho! call in the straggling few:
Much has been done, but much remains to do.
   Annawan.   Sachem,
Before thy face defeat muffles his own,
As if thy glance had turned him into stone.
   Totatomet. And at thy side the form of victory flies
To set thy name in glory's crimson skies.
   Warriors.   Ugh! ugh! ugh!
   Church. Philip, thy fortune like a rocket soars
And dazzles every eye with keen success;
But in the puddle of defeat will fall,

And sorrow's night will spread her wings o'er all.
Lothrop is dead, and his companions brave
Sleep in the dust; but from their timeless grave
Shall spring a spirit whose relentless hand
Torrents of blood shall pour on thy doomed land
In chastisement of this.
   Philip.   What ye will do
Is but a fœtus in the womb of time,
The midwife chance may never bring to life:
What we have done is written on men's minds
To live as long as they.—That other force
Unnecessary breathes the air: despatch
Braves to report their numbers and position:
Your ceaseless hands must usher them below.
                                      [*Exeunt.*

SCENE IV.—SOGKONATE. The Seconet Village. Enter in procession the Seconet squaws led by WENONAH, crowned with leaves and bearing in their hands the bladed cornstalks; they range in a circle, and sing to the music of rattle and drum beat by the medicine men.

THE CORN SONG.

I.

When from the cave of winter creeps
The month of leaves, and joyful leaps
    Nature at her new birth,
We plant thee in the mellow earth,
        Mondamin!

2.

The gentle dews sleep on thy bed ;
And when thou liftst thy silken head
    To bathe in tides of day,
Suns in pure gold thy limbs array,
        Mondamin !

3.

When wave thy green plumes in the air,
She, famed among the tribe most fair,
    Clothed in her naked charms,
Weaves spells to guard thy life from harms,
        Mondamin !

4.

At midnight hour she draws around
Circles of magic on the ground,
    Wherein no mildew blight
Hath power to pass, nor raven's flight,
        Mondamin !

5.

And when the month of falling leaves
Trees of their heritage bereaves,
    Maidens and young men strip
The armor from thy golden hip,
        Mondamin !

6.

Armor and spear to keep at bay
Death and his squadrons of decay,
    While howls the winter wind :
No friend like thee shall red men find,
        Mondamin !

Wenonah. Too many of our braves the foot of war
Have followed; in the pale-face eye it breaks
Our glass of loyalty. But there is one
No sentiment of honor, glory, pride,
Can prod to battle's arms. Ho, Samponcut!
   Samponcut. [*Within.*]   Ah-oh-ee!
   Wenonah.   Thou lazy bones,
Unclasp the form of slumber, and come forth.
   Wanda.   Unless thou notch a day
On the lodge pole, he'll sleep and know no loss.
   Samponcut. [*Within.*] Forbear, ye squaws!
   Wenonah.   Sweet Samponcut,
Divorce thine eyes from that proud sleep. See, the
   sun
With rosy feet walks o'er the panting waves!
Wampum grows in thy belt to rise betimes,
And drink the crystal stream of morning light.

           Enter SAMPONCUT.

   Samponcut.   What do I hear?
Divine wampum, present of the Manitou!
Born in the ocean, bred on earth to be
Giver of all good things, I worship thee!
   Wenonah.   Think if thou wert a brave,
And oared in glory's sea, thy hands would bear
Fathoms of this resolute friend.
                   [*Gives him wampum.*
   Samponcut. Oh, perfect belt, I wear thee in my
   heart!
A servant thou, silent, tireless, and true,
To do thy master's will. He shall but sit
In his grim lodge, and thou wilt take the world
Captive for him, and lay it at his feet.

His ragged back thy purple hand will hang
With the warm furs; and to the ends of earth
Travel to find, and down his stomach chase,
All luscious things.
 Wenonah.   No fruit in winter grows!
Fall on thy knees, and study there a prayer,
If holy thoughts the cave of thy low mind
May venture in.
 Samponcut. Why, why?
 Wenonah.   To teach thy joints,
Wrapped up in folds of birch-fed venison,
An honored path.
 Samponcut. I will experiment:
Pray the white Chief buffet with fortune's arm
The waves of war, and steer his bark of vows
In harbor of fidelity.
 Wenonah. No, no, no! If thou dost,
Both he and I are lost: some other theme.
 Samponcut. First tell me, Sachemess,
Why woman in her life the wide blue sea
Resembles.
 Wenonah. Because her heart is full of treasure.
 Samponcut. No reason there, Wenonah; try
  again.
 Wenonah. Oh, tell me in thy wisdom.
 Samponcut.   Because it is
Laden with craft.
    Enter ANUMPASH.
 Wenonah. A crafty answer. Look!
One back. Ah me! What of Pometacom?
 Anumpash. From triumph climbs to triumph,
  fresh and strong;
And dangers but salute and kneel to him.

Wenonah. What new exploit
On Squakeag treads?
Anumpash. Squaw,
Not thrice the sun's unwearied foot hath trod
That sapphire road, since he in ambush drew
An Essex regiment, and planted it
In death's sad field.
Wenonah. Where?
Anumpash. In the Nipmuck land.
Wenonah. Did none escape?
Anumpash. Upon thy fingers count
Them who slipped through the reeking hand of slaughter
Grown weary of its work.
Wenonah. My heart!
Samponcut. Oh rare Pokanoket!
Wenonah. Good Anumpash,
Tell me one thing.
Anumpash. Let the Squaw speak.
Wenonah. The pale-face chief of Aquidneck—
Thou knowest him?
Anumpash. Rugged he is, and tall,
As oak to forest trees.
Wenonah. Thou dost describe him well.
Anumpash. He hath an eye
In which the gloomy light of midnight waves
Welters; a brow whereon command doth sit;
And at his will no passion ever tugs.
Wenonah. Well, doth he live?
Anumpash. His fortune did outscowl
The eye of death: amid the balls that hailed
Their crimson storm, the bounty of the skies
Stood sentry to his life.

Wenonah.   Good Anumpash,
In my esteem thou art so richly clad
No faults of thine peer out upon the world.
And he escaped?
    Anumpash.   Escaped I did not say.
    Wenonah.   A captive then?
His freedom I will buy.
    Anumpash.   A captive, ay, but—
    Wenonah.   Ha!
    Anumpash.   But—
    Wenonah. I'll have no But, for in my eye it is
An unrepentant rebel, in defeat
Still plotting treason: let me hear it not.
    Anumpash.   I wed my lips to silence.
    Wenonah.   Who bid thee that?
    Anumpash.   My Chief!
    Wenonah.   Chain not thy tongue
In silence' cell, but saddle it with words
Of golden sound, and spur them in mine ear.
    Anumpash.   Then first I must unpack my present tale
And load my voice with fiction.
    Wenonah. Thou dost forget. It is of Church
I order thee to speak. Go on!
    Anumpash. But this: in hand of our Totatomet
The pale-face fell, and he is doomed to die.
    Wenonah.   How thy virtues fade
In my opinion's sun! A snow-man thou,
The churlish hands of winter in a night
On some charred stump fantastical had built,
To fright pappooses merely. I ungird
My good thoughts from thy name, and in the wind
Of cold displeasure set it. Get thee gone!

Anumpash. Henceforth I speak the truth in
    dreams alone ;
Never to women.   [*Exit.*
   Wenonah.   That liar, is he gone?
Bid him return!   [*Exit* WANDA.
                     His fortune had I gemmed
With pearls of favor, had his speech been more
Obedient to my wish.
   Samponcut.   Why stand him in rebuke
For others' deeds? On patience lean.
   Wenonah. He prates of patience who in fires of
    love
Hath never burned! Have I not seen and felt
Raging their stream of hate in triumph's hour?
The cruel honors paid to victory
In the dull groan ere yet the spirit leaps
Into that sea of night—the conqueror fire
Loading endurance' back with pelts and traps
Of unimagined woe that makes
All other falling but a midnight sleep.
Fast bound the prisoner stands so he can move
No arm nor leg, nor scarce the body writhe
When the rude arrows sow the shrinking flesh
With seeds of agony. The hatchets fly
Mindless to wound but lace the silver skin :
As whizzes through the air the uncouth steel,
The ecstasy of torture soars and soars ;
And camps in every chamber of the nerves
The mortal dew. Ages in minutes crowd,
When it may chance some young unpractised hand
With fatal aim will cast its tomahawk,
Crashing it in the unprotected brain ;

Then follow dismal yells as leap the braves
In headlong rush to tear the quivering scalp
Out at the roots.   Oh ! oh ! oh !

Re-enter WANDA.

Samponcut.   What says the brave ?
Wanda.   He will not come.
Samponcut.   Where is he ?
Wanda.   In his lodge
Oiling his locks with bear's grease, and his paint
A-scraping off.
Samponcut.   Soon will he gorge and sleep.
Wenonah.   Leave him to sullen thoughts,
And counsel me.
Samponcut.   Have I not heard a woman's tears
Softened Powhatan ?   To Pometacom
Go : if his nature be not changed by war,
For thee he will repeal this fiery law.
Wenonah.   I know he will ; for under friend-
   ship's tree
Our tribes have always dwelt.   We waste the time.
Quick, for my journey to Pokanoket
Prepare the needful things ; and I will seek
The Meda in his cave that he may shake
His sacred rattles, and so exorcise
Evil, and prosper my design.
Samponcut.   But wilt thou go alone ?
Wenonah.   Why not ?   I am the daughter of a
   chief,
In hardships drilled and follower of grief ;
And chartered as a warrior's chosen bride
To tread the path of danger at his side.
Samponcut.   Force makes the better plea.

Wenonah.   Let fifty braves
Camp on my trail.
   Samponcut.   Totatomet must answer this.
   Wenonah.   If he escape the lightning blast,
The heavens are guilty.
                         [*Exeunt all but* SAMPONCUT.
   Samponcut. That welkined love! A hurricane it is
Bends trees of opposition 'neath its breath,
Tears up and flings aside all noxious growths
Of thou-shalt-not that rankle in its path;
A flame in which each sort and class of men
Melt in that lava state of doubt and hope,
Elation, sorrow, that knock round the heart
Unanchored like a shell on the free waves.
No gibble-gabble for thee, friend Samponcut!
Shake thou the hand of time for that the snow
Sprinkles thy hair, and all thy blood is cold:
Else should some doting lead thee in the trap
Set by the dimpled one, while lords of wit
Fattened their gibes and sneers at thy weak legs
Marched to and fro, here and there, up and down,
To do the bidding of some tanned delight
Who in the end might shake scorn's icy drops
Upon the tender petals of thy love.   [*Exit.*

ACT III.

SCENE I. POKANOKET. The Wampanoag village.

Rude music. Enter PHILIP, ANNAWAN, AGAMAUG, ALDERMAN, CANONCHET, QUINNAPIN, MONOKO, TUSPAQUIN, TATOSON, POMHAM, *and warriors with* CHURCH *and other captives on one side; on the other, Wampanoag squaws headed by* WOOTONEKANUSKE, *chanting a scalp song.*

THE SCALP SONG.

1.

See where the brave in triumph come
Proudly to note of fife and drum,
    With firm, defiant tread :
The crop of foes that grew around
They sickled on a bloody ground,
    A harvest of the dead !

    Hail to the hero band !
    Pride of the Kinshon land,
    Who, valor hand in hand,
    Girded with glory stand.

2.

With scalps their girdles thick are hung ;
Over their brawny shoulders flung
    The trophies of the slain :
Rewards are theirs the noble prize ;
And songs that climb the smiling skies
    In no penurious strain.

Hail! hail! the victors hail!
Braves shall in terror quail,
Squaws shall for mercy wail,
When ye your foes assail.

3.

But some in arms of death asleep
Our fruitful eyes shall ever weep,
   And comfort strangled be;
For in their lodge deject and drear
Famine will stalk with hideous leer,
   And life in anguish flee.

Guard ye the desolate
Beset by fires of fate!
So shall the Spirit Great
Your triumphs vindicate.

[*Exeunt some of the braves leading the prisoners, followed by squaws and pappooses who hoot and jeer them, and brandish knives and hatchets in their faces.*

Wootonekanuske.   Pometacom!
Philip.   My dear squaw!
Wootonekanuske.   What joy
Travels in my sad heart when I again
Hang on thy lips, and raise these shadowed eyes
Up in thy face.
   Philip.   This moment pays the debt
Of that poor time, and gives me a discharge
From regiment of grief.
   Wootonekanuske.   Yet could I drink
Those bitter days again, to be but so.

PHILIP OF POKANOKET. 61

Philip. Oneka, sorrows thou hast borne,
Ills of so giant size my worst of days
Were pigmies in their eye. Why did I feel
Happy, when thou wert not!
    Wootonekanuske.   Dear Metacom,
Give them no thought.
    Philip.   Nay, speak;
For in my breast there roams no sentiment
But turns at last to thee.
    Wootonekanuske. Driven from swamp to swamp,
At night I lay me in a hollow tree;
Or crouching in the arms of savage rocks
Where bears inhabit, wooed the fall of sleep
To whelm my bark of cares.
    Philip.   For every pang
They racked thee on, Pometacom will lay
A settlement in ashes.
    Wootonekanuske. For food I searched
The fallen pines in net of slow decay
Tangled, on whose black breast lift up their heads
Red wintergreens, and beat into a pulp
Plantain and dock, and scooped the crystal spring
Washing the rock's mossed face, from famine's hand
To lock my life.
    Philip.   Heart of ruth!
In no hour when treading the sunless wilds,
Bivouacked on star-lit hills, or victory's bowl
Draining of blood, hath thy companionship
Been absent from my mind. And now I come
In triumph robed, and deafed with glory's voice
That sets my fame on such a pinnacle,
Oblivion's hand may never pull it down,—
To bid a prouder fortune kneel to thee;

And every grain of care sown on thy brow
Plough out with love.

Wootonekanuske.   To see this much-longed day
When climbs thy wave on fortune's smiling shore,
All sorrow that hath feasted on my heart,
And all the future holds, chameleon-like,
Changes to joy.

Enter METACOMET.

Philip.   No more am I
The servant of desire!—Metacomet!
Let me peruse the volume of thy face,
To learn the lines of mine when first a boy
In rapture I did bend the sinewy bow
To lance the cheek of air.   It fathers me
With a new joy, and with a pleasing fear,
To hold thee in mine arms, and see thine eyes
Flash in the light of mine.   Where hast thou been?

Metacomet.   In the black swamps, Sachem.
Philip.   What to do?
Metacomet. To lurk under the hemlock's shaggy arms, and shoot mine arrows at the dismal crows.
Philip.   Nor feared the Umpames?
Metacomet. A Wampanoag is not a brother to fear.
Philip. My spirit dwells in thee! The nation, boy,
Will huddle all its honors on thy back,
And chieftain thee, if thou wilt always spurn
The knee of fear, and grow to my desire:
A sachem shalt thou be, and at thy voice
The forest tenantry will leap to arms,
And every lodge untreasure.

[*They retire apart.*

Quinnapin. Nay, nay, nay!

Monoko. I will wager my string of scalps to a bundle of rushes that the belly of his valor is so crammed with unbolted fears that on the next trail he will hug close the fireside of his lodge, and digest in the sun of idleness the perilous food of war thrust down the throat of his courage.

Quinnapin. Thy string of scalps! How many of them didst thou harvest in a foeman's skull; and how many have since been halved and quartered by thy new device to take our admiration prisoner? I would teach my tongue some discretion.

Monoko. Teach thy lechery discretion! Then wilt thou not be chased out of a mistaken lodge by an irate brave, and be forced to swear thou camest by thy wounds in a midnight skirmish with the pale-faces, to thread the eye of thy squaw's suspicions.

Quinnapin. May the Great Spirit hear him! Thy face alone would strip a wigwam of its inmates, by merely peering under the deerskin: nothing shall you see there to subdue the virtue of our squaws.

Annawan. Nushkah! these pestilent knaves will quarrel with their own shadows; with the impertinent wind because it drops a leaf upon the forest trail; with the golden-rod because its color does not match the sky. An Pometacom slap not the face of occasion and give them the cud of another war to chew upon, their blood will chafe these banks of idleness till it overflow our peace in constant broils.

Monoko. A war for him, my father! No! he holds his blood too precious to smear that fluid on the arm of valor. Let a mosquito but sluice out of his veins a rivulet of red, he bellows like a calf and blubbers that his last hour is come.

Alderman. It was the only cloud on victory's sky. Say how it fell.

Agamaug. It came about in this way. Many of the Nipmucks stood aloof, and dieted their love of Pometacom with fears of the various bodies of pale-faces stationed on the river: they dreaded that his good fortune would stumble in so steep an enterprise. But when Squakeag had stooped the head of defiance; when Deerfield had been garmented in flames, and bands of whites in all directions ambushed and cut to pieces, then the Nipmuck chiefs no longer drank the fountain of neutrality. They dug up the hatchet; unbarred their gate to three hundred of our braves: we trod in thought on ruins of Springfield. That flower blossomed not: the icy hand of treachery untimely nipped the bud of our project. Toto—whose name be buried in the grave of infamy!—revealed the plot: our torrent beat against their garrison in vain. But fire betrayed us not: their homes and barns were clasped to its red breast, and that did comfort us.

Alderman. Yet say that Toto for his fit reward Sups in the dust.

Agamaug. His face is yet Familiar with the sun.

Canonchet. Is there no hand in service to the cry Age-honored, that a renegade must die?

Pomham. Had I his throat between these hands
   of mine,
With Mitchi-Manitou the wretch would dine.
   Tuspaquin. Within his lodge come never veni-
      son ;
No wampum breed beneath his guilty hand ;
Nor age camp on his brow !
   Tatoson. But vengeance shall outstrip the trai-
      tor's crime,
Though it may travel slow and take its time ;
And even while the messenger delays
Remorse still on the villain's conscience preys ;
For in his mind a thousand deaths he dies,
Ere to his heart the fatal arrow flies.
   Quinnapin. I would the conscience of that Nip-
muck should upbraid him for the enticement of
much wampum out of my wigwam, the which I
loved as the she-bear loves her cubs ; but if such
stalk grew in his soil, it hath been thrice wilted
in the sun of depravity till there is no unshrivelled
arm to hang a good resolution on.
   Monoko. My heart is the same color as my face.
His only friends are the population of his hair
whom he petitions with his nails to visit his stomach : he fears to hunt his food.
   Annawan. The marrow burn your bones ! Will
ye ever rub the sore of your disputes with words,
words, words !
   Philip. Be ever pupil to those valiant thoughts !
But see, the chiefs !
   Canonchet.   Pometacom,
The sun behind the rosy clouds of eve
Stables his golden steeds, and bids us go.

Philip. Have ye the spoil
Parted? Is each one satisfied? For then,
Feed on my share.
    Canonchet. If our desires
Had swelled like mountain brooks in April time,
Thy bounty would have dwarfed them all.
    Philip. It tries to reach to your deserts.
Yet words of praise but limp behind your deeds,
Too slow to overtake them. In the face
Of giant wrongs you threw rebellion's glove;
And though your steps were tangled in the fears
Thick-growing in the hearts of lukewarm tribes;
Though discipline was weeded from your ranks
By liberty's rough hand, and treachery's teeth
Mangled the form of darling enterprise;
Yet over all your active courage climbed,
And on the hills and peaks of victory
Planted your arms.
    Warriors. Ugh! ugh! ugh!
    Pomham. Chief, to our lodges we will take
These bright-haired scalps, and on their tresses
    read,
In lines of fire, triumphs to come.
    Quinnapin. What sayest thou? Survives a sad-
    eyed white
Monoko's hand plunged not in endless night?
    Monoko. Pometacom, he swims in mirth,
But on the war-path, nothing worth.—
Pray for a magic wand in a tree's rind
Viewless to render thee when the braves chant
The mortal song.
    Philip. Brothers, not all that human field
Have ye yet reaped. The conquests ye have made

Are garrisoned by ruin, your captives bound
In silent forts of death : them that yet live,
Whose breathing yet offends the sacred air,
We next push in the sea.
   Warriors.   Ugh ! ugh ! ugh !
   Philip.   As thunder drops
On guilty heads, and sullen stalks away,
Its mission ended, ye have scourged your foes
As swift and terrible. Your fathers' bones
Gloat in their shrouds of clay ; and where he dwells
In undecaying lodge, the Manitou
Smiles, well-contented, on his children's deeds.
But if be born a time when enterprise
Stumbles in path of unity, defeat,
Black-browed, will rise and tear out of your hands
The fruit of former toils. Be sure, my braves,
Our freedom is begirt with loose decay,
If faction quarrel with authority.
The snake of discord throttle at its birth,
Lest it shall grow a monster in whose sting
Poison resides to canker up the blood,
And choke the swelling veins of sovereign sway,
Our cause diseasing. On that golden face
Lives no reproach. If, moccasined with flame,
He lead us back the pleasant month of leaves,
And see you perfect, over this forest realm
Where pale-faces unkennel dogs of change,
I swear the red man shall forever range.
   Warriors. Mugwump! Mugwump! Mugwump!
   Canonchet.   Wampanoag, thou art a man
Whose words and deeds have ever kept abreast.
When left the sun his wigwam in the south
And travelled north, he saw a hundred towns

Where dwelt the whites in happiness and power.
Now where he casts his eye he but beholds
Ruin and death. We have not strength to bear
Our heavy pole of scalps ; no more for blood
Our hatchets thirst. Yet as it is thy will,
We drive revenges in our mind again.
  Philip.   Canonchet,
Our foot hath merely bruised the serpent's head :
He'll coil him up, and strike his venomed fang.
The deer will not come back where pale-face smoke
Sullies the sky, and lays the forest low.
But oil your bow strings in the shrouded light
Of six more moons, that so your steps may roam
In freedom over every hill and dale.
  Canonchet. It is our only wish.

  [*Exeunt all but* Philip, Annawan, Wootonekanuske, *and* Metacomet.

  Annawan.   Pometacom,
When shall we bring that pale-face to the stake ?
  Philip. Not now, good Annawan. I find my heart
Swimming in tide of gentle thoughts, to bank
Of deep content. Leave him awhile.
  Annawan. To-morrow it shall be. His life offends
The eye of my delight.
  Philip.   Nay, let us cool our hate
With moderation's breath. Have we not all ?
Oneka, come !   [*Exeunt.*

SCENE II.—SOGKONATE. A cove partly sheltered by
a thin clump of low pines.

   SAMPONCUT, *fitting out a canoe.*

 Samponcut. No spirits in the bold light of these
  days
Travel the earth to do their weary tasks
When men are sleeping!
      These are dainties fit
For one enskyed. No snails and earth worms
  mashed
In a vile jelly which your Puritan
Crams down his children's throat, but viands fair,
Tribute of land and sea. White oysters there,
Fattened in the still depths by ocean's hand;
Here, sober clams that carry on their back
A house of purple shell; sand-loving snipe;
Ear-corn roasted in ashes of red oak.
But she's in love, and not a morsel sweet
Will pass her lips.

   Enter TOTATOMET.

    Now the Manitou
Unknits his brow!
 Totatomet. It drives
Grief from the bosom of Totatomet,
To grasp this wrist again.
 Samponcut.   Dwell I in lodge of dream
With all thy limbs intact! No, not a wound
The magic of proud victory hath not healed,
Ere yet the notes of battle died on air.
These pledges to thy worth an homage pay,
And hem thy belt with glory. One, two, four,

Six, eight, ten! Pride of the Seconets,
While parched our lives in their inglorious bower,
Thy fortune sprouted in a golden shower.
 Totatomet. Father,
It washed our hands with riches.
 Samponcut.   That Chief!
His wondrous story mocks a meda's tale
Told by the fire. Reports of your success
Followed upon each other's heels so fast,
Before our wonder could digest the first
A next would choke its throat.
 Totatomet. Ay, Samponcut, it was as though
Mischance were lamed and limped behind, or fell
Before his glance; as if desiring food
We had but shot our arrows in the air,
Aimless and wild, and lo! the unseen deer
Panted on earth.
 Samponcut. My matchless brave! But in thine
   eye
What dulness dwells. Still dost thou stagger
   there?
 Totatomet. Dear Samponcut,
I plunged into this war as in a sea
To drown those thoughts; but faithful memory
Will ever pluck them up. How fares the Squaw?
 Samponcut. How did the Red Swan fare
When in her breast the magic arrow flew?
 Totatomet. I follow not.
 Samponcut.   Deeply she pines
Since fortune to captivity betrayed
The whiskered one.
 Totatomet. Her thoughts still hold a truce with
   him!

Samponcut.   Ay, in her bay of love
His vessel rides, so sheltered and secure,
No wave of separation, no wind of time,
May drive it hence.
   Totatomet.   But I will raise a storm
Shall shatter on the shoals and rocks of grief
Her and her utmost hopes.   Mine she must be.
   Samponcut.   Exile the wish!   The Sachemess is
      proud,
Stubborn, and hath a will not to be mined
By thy desires.
   Totatomet.   Ride to death
Thy quibbles, Samponcut: in serious path
Journeys my thought.   From youth thou knowest
      me :
Grew aught on branch of possibility
But I did climb to it?
   Samponcut.   Nay, failure doth not grow
Under thy clime—I mean, it is not writ
In any wampum thine.   Unfold thy plan.
   Totatomet.   Walk then in the straight path.
A prisoner in my hands the pale-face lies.
Yoked to his new offence of loving her,
An ancient grudge I bear him from a suit
Growing, in Plymouth to recover lands
Beguiled from me when drink had made my mind
Captive to folly ; and I hate him now
Doubly, for that by liked gifts and by words
More eloquent than in my tongue reside,
The favor in Wenonah's eyes I held,
He throws a tarnish on.   Pometacom
Is friendly to my purpose he shall burn
In triple fires.   If yet he drinks the air

'Tis so I may wring from that beauty's heart
Cold drops of horror, and behold her face
Droop in despair when I make known his fate
Beyond reprieve, ere thrice that golden foot
Treads the soft blue, his limbs are clad in death.

    Samponcut.   But she knows this,
For Anumpash is here, and hath revealed
Thy dismal plans. And so, at her command,
Freighted is this canoe to bear her soon
Hence to Pokanoket, when she will melt
The Sachem's heart with pity and remorse
To free the white.

    Totatomet. Ha! is it so? Quick! bring me where
Her summer wigwam stands.

    Samponcut.   Not I, sweet Seconet!
But if thy courage would her fury brave,
When evening falls seek thou Pambassa's cave.
She goes to test the holy Meda's skill
Within the future's book to read the will
Of the Great Spirit.

    Totatomet.   It is full an hour
Before the wearied warrior of the sky
Takes off his gleaming arms. Until that time,
At thy good board, thy company shall lend
Mine ear discourse of the events that fell
While I beneath the Nipmuck skies did dwell.

    Samponcut. Why, to be sure! No more are we content
To feed on fame alone!   [*Exeunt.*

SCENE III.—SOGKONATE. The Cave of Pambassa, its rocky walls hung with pipes, rattles, and medicine bags. On one side a gourd lamp on a shelf of stone; on the other, a couch of skins.

Enter TOTATOMET.

Totatomet. I am in time. The night is pure
    serene ;
Her darkling form swims through the tides of space
With gentlest motion. On the heaving waves,
With silver feet, the moon in beauty walks.
Down in her cataract of splendor sink
The dwindled lanterns of the common stars,
Which in her absence hang their solemn lights
On heaven's ramparts. So doth every grace
Blink its weak eye before Wenonah's face.
The lord of light in his long march on high,
Never hath seen a creature that can vie
On terms with her. And shall the pale-face snatch
Those charms no beauty of his race can match ?
Out of these veins let hooded vampires sluice
My molten blood, unto my soul lay siege
Hosts of dismay, battalions of remorse,
When I forbid it not.—
    Pambassa, ho !—
I had thought to tread out this flame, and make
A counsellor of pride, but absence fed
Still more the wasting fire. My Manitou !
I have him in my power. At my command
Wanders his shadow in the spirit land.—
    What ho ! Pambassa, ho !—
He sleeps—'tis well. In the uncertain light
This moss like snowy locks will seem ; his robe

5

That wrapped the Meda's form ere I was born,
Will speak of him—so, so. Now if I use
A halting gait, and let a rasping cough
Dwell in my throat—uh, uh, uh—that will do.
But hark! a step upbraids the quiet night.
Down on those skins beyond the flickering light.
Uh, uh, uh!

          Enter WENONAH.

  Wenonah.   Pambassa, art thou here?
  Totatomet.   Who thus disturbs
The slumbers of a dying man? Uh, uh, uh!
  Wenonah. I am Wenonah, and it grieves my heart
Thou art unwell. In pity of thy state,
I have hung at thy door a wampum belt
Shall purchase thee all simples of the woods,
To lead thee back to health.
  Totatomet.   I know thee now,
And thank this malady that sets ajar
The door of death, that so these fading eyes
Born in the glory of my Sogkonate,
May never see its fall. Uh, uh, uh!
  Wenonah.   So strange thy words,
I know them not.
  Totatomet.   Art thou not she
Who, by alliance with the pale-face race
Red men divorce forever from their love,
Hath bathed the honors of the Seconets
In river of disgrace?
  Wenonah.   Listen, Pambassa.
  Totatomet. I do remember thee. Thou art th
  one

Whose love is of a quality so strange,
It could not harbor in our native stream,
But journeyed far in quest of new delights,
And feasted on a foe.
    Wenonah.   Should such a charge
Go with my life?
    Totatomet.   Thou wilt deny it not.
The thunder birds are angry, and the crow
Caws from the blasted pine his dismal note.
When rose the voice of the Wampanoag
Horsed on the blasts of war, and the stern tribes
It marshalled to the conflict followed on,
Like wave to wave, the hand that should have led,
Turned back the current of our discontent
In the scum pool of peace. What dost thou here?
    Wenonah.   Father, thou art ill.
A dark spirit hath entered in thy breast,
And robbed thee of thy voice and thine old ways;
For both of them to what I knew them once,
Are of no kin.
    Totatomet.   Uh, uh, uh, uh!
'Tis thou art changed—not I.
Daughter, I love thee. When I love thee not,
These ninety years, the mellow fruit of time,
Drop in the mouth of death! But hearken thou:
The ear of ancient manners is abused
By thy new life.
Before, thou wert a votaress of my praise,
Drinking my counsel as the leaf the dew;
But now a strangeness hath unknit the coil
That bound unto my holy oracles
Thy patient days.
A snake hath slyly crept amid our tribe,

Leaving the slime of his detested thoughts
To smear the tender blade of thy resolves.
His forkèd tongue a venom hath distilled
Into thy mind to make it loathe our ways,
And lead it 'neath the roof of foreign laws,
The Seconets condemning.

    Wenonah.   If I have erred,
In love of Sogkonate I did it all.

    Totatomet.   With duty's show
We often fringe the cloak of our desires.

    Wenonah.   Ah, pity me!
I am unhappy, father, and I came
Thy counsel to implore. The pale-face chief
Is growing in the garden of my heart:
Remonstrances are vain to tear him out
My soil of love. But now misfortune's hand
Delivers him to the Wampanoag
Whose sea of hate will swallow up his life.
If thou hast ever held my totem dear,
Pray that I may redeem him from the fire.

    Totatomet.   My child,
Seek not to change the Manitou's design.
Nay, bid me rattle the harsh gourd and sing
Ha-he-hi-hah, and exorcise thine imp;
Or make of him a figure in pine bark,
And place it at the door for our young men
To shoot their arrows at. Shake off this love.
Curb not the fiery heart of Sogkonate
Whose spirit frets against these bars of peace,
And censures thee. Say to that alien race
That urges thee to stab our brother's hope,
Ye milk the ram, and to you we can be
But instruments of death. From thy thought's wall

Tear down the image of that soon-no-more
Pale-face who turned thy reason inside out,
Dressing the worst in garb of the best cause;
And in thy favor hang that brave of braves,
Totatomet. The god is speaking.

Wenonah. Methinks a devil speaks, and not a god.
The frayed and ravelled suit of him whose name
Never again will march upon my tongue,
Is cast off, and no words may weave it up.
I would abhor to lay on me a yoke
So to subdue the resolute heart I bear.
My soul is free as air, and as the sea
Boundless, and ever shall its love bestow,
False priest, on whom it please, and when, and
    where.

Totatomet. Poison that in the mandrake
Dwells, blow thy blood! Now patience from my
    breast
Exiled shall be; and on thy desperate will
Ride rude command. Know I am one
              [*Throwing off his disguise.*
Whose enterprise bends not its stately head
To foot of faltering. Squaw, to my lodge
Now thou must go!

Wenonah. [*Recoils in horror.*] Totatomet!

Totatomet. Think not to 'scape my hand.
I have in this the warrant of the tribe;
And thy disdain shall balk it not.

Wenonah. Back! back! I say, unworthy Seco-
    net;
And with no touch profane me.

Totatomet. Yield thee, Squaw.

Chafe not the swollen current of my blood
Which else shall break in fury through thy bar.
   Wenonah?   Brave, art thou mad?
Put up thy knife, or turn it on thyself,
Such treason's grim and old-time penalty.
      [*He shrinks back overawed by her looks.*
Ay, let it search the caverns of thy breast
With murderous hands, and where it finds thy heart
House in it deep as death. I fear thee not.
   Totatomet. Then fear for him, the jewel of thy soul
Torn from its prosperous setting by my hand.
Deep shalt thou drain the hot and bitter cup
Thy folly brews, while the face of thy proud thoughts
Grovels in ashes of remorse. Bethink,
My haughty Squaw, now lighted is the fire
Whose crimson jaws all greedy shall lick up
His sizzling stream of flesh. I will be there;
And I will teach the eager knots of pine
The lexicon of hate from A to Z,
So anguish on him peer with hellish looks;
And tell him she who flattered him with love,
Is author of his woe. Proud woman-chief,
Already do I hear, and so mayst thou,
The groans that split his heart, and drag it down
Abysses of despair and gulfs of woe,
Till it shall riot in such agony,
In wildness and in frenzy he will call
The still and gracious death.   [*Exit.*
   Wenonah.   What have I done?
Betrayed him to his death? No, no, no, no!

Fetters that Seconet can never forge
My credit with the great Chief may not break.
His threats but arm me in my new design
With stronger resolution. I will pray
That all is well, but oh ! how cold 'tis here.
Ere the Great Bear under the starry pole
Crouches, I must be gone. Pometacom
When he struck the war-post did never bid
Farewell to mercy. Under his cold mien
A lenient nature flows. He will stamp out
The cruelty of the other.—Samponcut !—
No monsters lurk in the dark ocean caves
Fierce as a lover scorned.—Ho, Samponcut !
                                                      [*Exit.*

ACT IV.

SCENE I.—POKANOKET. The Wampanoag village. A council of chiefs: ANNAWAN, TUSPAQUIN, TATOSON, ALDERMAN, and AGAMAUG. Braves and squaws.

Annawan.   Where is the Seconet?
Agamaug. The path between your village and
    his lodge
Is not a short one, Annawan.
Annawan.   He should be here to taint
This rawest fancy of Pometacom
With a hot opposition.
Tuspaquin.   Nay, let the Sachem pluck
This plume from mercy's wing: enough remains.
Annawan.   Nushkah! had I my wish at one
    black stake
Would I bind every white whose foot hath scorched
The red man's land, upon the wings of flame
Waft them away.
Alderman.   The Sachem's heart is soft:
When mercy knocks his kindness takes her in.
Annawan.   I wish to die before my heart is soft.
He is the bravest, wisest of the whites,
And his escape revives the drooping stalk
Of their bad cause. Only his death can bolt
Our door of safety.

Enter PHILIP.

Tatoson.   The Sachem comes.

Philip. All hath been settled save the fate of him
Whose valor anchors in our stream of love
His forfeit life. Kekamah, bring him in!
                                           [*Exit a brave.*
I think thee, Alderman, thy brother's shade :
The grave alone can part you.
    Alderman.   No, my chief,
Not even that.
    Philip.   Hi, hi, your friendship's eye
Outstares the love of women.—

              Church *is led in.*

                        Set him there! Chiefs,
If he will bolster up his wounded lot
With pillow of our life, shall we refuse
To taste the fruit?—
Pale-face, what hath thy dauntless soul to say
Why death should not inherit now thy clay?
    Church. It is the chance of war : I am content.
    Philip. Thy heart is brave, never to danger
        bent.
Foremost in ranks of battle hast thou fought ;
And in life's sea the pearl of honor sought.
That life, unlike thy false perfidious race,
The garment of an honest heart doth lace ;
And though thy musket hath our death-song sung,
Our justice grants thou art no double-tongue.
    Church. Philip, I thank thee. If my race be
        run,
Dying, I own in fairest combat won.
    Philip.   White Chief,
Large ransom hath been offered for thy life
Won by Totatomet in equal strife ;

But he, choked by the fumes of hatred deep,
Freely can breathe but in thine endless sleep.
His prisoner thou; but means are in my power,
If so I will, to stay thy fatal hour.
    Church.   I listen to thy words, Wampanoag.
    Philip.   Pale-face,
The red man's life is dignified and free:
We worship one above and—liberty.
Our forest towns no moats, no ramparts pen;
But guarded by a living wall of men
They stand. Our streets no thieves, no beggars
    tread.
In our domain no jail lifts up its head.
For others' ease no lowly classes toil:
All live joint tenants of the common soil.
    Warriors.   Ugh! ugh! ugh!
    Philip.   Pale-face,
The sickle of this war hath mowed our braves
In swaths of blood down to their timeless graves;
But not in vain—never, I say, in vain:
For where their forms stalk through the sullen
    tomb,
Four pale-face spirits glad them in the gloom.
We welcome to our ranks the manly heart
Who at our feast of glory craves a part.
Thine is an arm in valor's eye so dear,
Our tribes give it the worship of their fear.
In this wide world thou standest now alone,
Thy fate in hands where mercy is unknown.
But shall we squander in the greedy grave
The wealth of prowess would our fortunes lave
In triumph's sea, enlisted in our cause?
Or shall we say: submit thee to our laws;

Come to our lodges, free, embrace our life;
Among our black-haired daughters take a wife:
A chieftain be, and at our council-fire
Hear thy voice honored like the tribal sire?

[*Confused cries from the band, some in approval, others in opposition.*]

    Annawan.   Cram down his throat
A fist of dust!
    Philip.   A cup of calmness drain!—
Pale-face, bethink thee if our mercy throw
This rope of safety, wouldst thou clutch at it?
    Church.   What's that?
Wandered my thoughts in fields of happier days.
If it be nothing that will strip my faith
Naked to the world's shrewd blast, I will lead
Mine inclinations in it.
    Philip.   Thou must become as one of us.
Each fort of old affection and regard
Must be dismantled, and forgetfulness
Creep over them; thy zeal and purposes
Cry "Hail" to our resolves; what we decide
Graft on thy will; say to thy former self
A last good-night; and all the freight of hope
Thy bosom bears, land on our shore.
    Church.   Ha! ha! ha!
    Philip. Why dost thou laugh?
    Church.   And if I say:
Pokanoket, I will do this, and so
Hoodwink suspicion, till I pluck a chance
Out of occasion's hand to shake thy dust
From off my feet, shall I not then be free?

Philip.   The penalty is death
But to attempt it.
     Church.   Lip-service is not mine.
Philip, I cannot marry to thy tribe
Warring with mine and in their curses set,
My true devotion. Let it end.
     Philip.   Pale-face, on no slight cause
Pull down thy mortal house.
     Church. Tempter, away! Should I with dull
          apostasy
Mangle my early creed, baptize mine arms
Most foully in my dear companions' blood,
Would they not set a stigma on my name,
And shake my memory from their branch of love?
Or if they should condone my deepest fall,
And dredge mine honor out of treason's sea,
How shall I answer to the inward voice?
Can I flee from it to the haunts of men;
Or in the noblest school of solitude
Plead poverty of will? All would be vain!
It would pursue me with unflagging step
Around the earth; embitter every hour;
And make a grave seem gentle place of rest.
Teach me another way.

           Enter TOTATOMET.

    Philip. I know of none.
    Totatomet.   Come, let the fire
Feel for his heart.
    Philip.   Art thou resolved
To court this darkness?
    Church.   I think of what I am,
Sachem, and it forbids my faltering now.

Hast thou not heard, I have a vow in heaven
Recorded in the angel's book where I
Turn every day my thought to read it there.
That oath was sworn above the mangled forms
Of all my dear below, where they were found
In ruins of our home, the satan work
Of redskins such as ye, when they let loose
Hell on the earth. If I a compact seal
With thy destruction, from these sides would rot
Mine arms forsworn, and on my perjured head
The lightning fall. No, Philip, no!
 Alderman. If Providence hath no spies out,
Minutes may span his rivulet of life.
 Agamaug.   I see his limbs
Mantled in fire.
 Annawan. I thank the Manitou
I see this day, if it be so!
 Church. Oh Sogkonate! what happiness
Circled thy name!—No, Philip, I may not
Unclothe my character to that bleak change.
Thou mayst but try me to my fall, then pour
Contempt and laughter on me. I will strive
To guide me by the chart the rarest use
In desert of our life; cling to my cross,
Clad in a mood that throttles accidents
And binds the feet of change.
 Philip.   Thou must not say
I jested with thy state; but if thou mask
Under this choice a purpose to escape,
Strangle the thought. Yet if thou hast to ask
Aught that the gorge and stomach of our place
May not strain at, let me but hear.
 Church. My fortune has not run, Wampanoag,

Along with thine, but stumbled by the way.
Renown and triumph wait upon thy steps,
And flatter thee with visions of a time
When all the settlements shall prostrate lie
Ruined, beneath thine arm ; the thirsty earth
Lap up the blood of the last colonist ;
While o'er the sites where they have reared their
    homes,
The green foot of the old primeval woods
In silence creeps. Sachem, let not thy thought
Follow such false trail, an unskilled hunter there.
Soon is this voice the bride of silence ; hence
A prophecy sits in my final words :
The Saxon face is set against the sun,
And follows where his golden steeds do run.
Disasters have but built our purpose strong
Rather to perish than submit to wrong.
Yet have we not put forth our latent power ;
The lion in us hath not had his hour ;
But when we rise in all our might of wrath
Swept are our foes like chaff before our path.
    Annawan.   Thy boasting now !
    Warriors.   To the stake ! to the stake !
    Philip. Thy weakness shall be passport to thy
        tongue
To pass the sentinel of modest doubt.
Pale-face, I friended thee and put a staff
Into thy hands to lead thee out of death ;
But thou hast held thee on a different way,
Saluting not the face of my design.
The braves they say thy life is forfeited.
No fault is mine : thy blood be on thy head !
    Warriors.   To the stake ! to the stake !

Church. Words will but spend my fleeting
    breath in vain.
A renegade, my name would die amain;
But dying faithful it shall live again.
              [*Exit, between the guards.*
Philip. Totatomet, be thine to set the stake.
Brave Seconet, much do we owe thine arm :
To-night thy hate embraces its revenge.
    Totatomet. Thy thanks do set a glory on my
        deeds.   [*Exeunt.*

SCENE II.—POKANOKET. An open space in the centre
    of the Wampanoag village, with a stake set up sur-
    rounded by fagots and brushwood. Time, night;
    around, pine knots throw a lurid light.

Enter PHILIP, ANNAWAN, TOTATOMET, TATOSON, AGA-
    MAUG, ALDERMAN, *warriors and squaws.*

    Philip. Nay, policy was parent of that wish :
So true a branch engrafted on our tree
Had dropped us fruit of choicest victory.
    Annawan. Better this way. The braves for
        vengeance cry,
And with one voice demand the pale-face die.
The red men's blood his ruthless hand hath shed
Forms in a cloud to burst upon his head;
And freer shall we breathe when such a foe,
Harmless for aye, sits with the shades below.
    Philip. It likes me not to bathe in useless blood.
To no man will my mounting spirit yield
When battle rages in the crimson field;

But when his wings are drooped in victory,
From savage thoughts my mind is purged and free.
   Annawan.   Pometacom,
Wilt thou not own this gift is due thy tribe ;
And due the allies who have spent their blood
To purchase thee dominion ?
   Philip.   .   Good Annawan,
Their minds dyed in the vat of our fierce trade,
Hold not the scales in which my thoughts are
     weighed.
The present moment bounds their little day,
Moulding their souls beneath its tyrant sway.
   Annawan. Hast thou forgot how oft the whites
     betrayed
The character of justice they parade ?
Our braves when captured in the stricken field,
Do they to mercy or to ransom yield ?
Ask of the winds that kiss the trunkless heads
Grimly their hellish hands nail up on poles
To guard the reeking gates of Plymouth town !
Ask of the waves dandling in azure arms
The guilty prows that speed across the seas,
Bearing our brothers, squaws, and pappooses
To hopeless bondage in the red-skyed south
Where life is bound in caves of bitterness !
Nushkah ! mercy shown to such as these is crime
To thee and thine, and mocks the austere time.

         Enter TUSPAQUIN.

   Philip. What news comes on thy haste ?
   Tuspaquin.   The Plymouth father sends
A flag of truce, and offers to exchange
Ten red men for the life of Captain Church.

This failing, they will make our brothers' breast
A grave for lead, and sell the captured squaws
Slaves in that land where sleeps the winter sun.
Besides, he has called out all that remain
Of young and old to gird their armor on;
Recruits from Shawmut begs, and all the towns
Spared by the fire, with frenzied hands to roll
Back our great wave; the while on bended knees
He prays the bullet into Philip's heart.
 Philip. The white flag back, and let me see
Nothing but red! I from this moment tear
All softness from my nature, and will be
Hard as the granite, hungry as the sea.
 Annawan. Have I not said!
 Philip. Enough! He shall not live another day
Lest deeper wrongs our weak forbearance pay.
What ho! the prisoner!

    CHURCH *is led in.*
   Now bind him, braves.
     [*He is bound to the stake.*
 Totatomet. Use no weak thongs!
 Agamaug. His looks are downcast, and his mind
  is dyed
Pensive, to color of his poor condition.
 Alderman. This is the test
That writes his name on pages of the air,
Or carves it on tradition's stone.
 Tatoson. Listen!
He prays in low voice to his nation's god
Whose arm can aid him nevermore.
 Church. Alack the day! How ill my sternness
  weighed

The body's power to stand against that sleet
Of torture, bruising and beating down to shame
The tendrils of the will: the gauntlet run
Down that black avenue with wild-eyed beasts
Lined, whose clubs like fire-stones pelted my back,
Till fortitude stooped to the foot of anguish!
Oh God! thy grace supplant my feeble will
Bound captive to the chariot of pain;
And like a rock beat back the grievous surge
That saps this fort, for worse assault must come!
Thou light and refuge in the night of life,
Send from the heaven of heavens where thou
    dost sit
Enthroned in pity with the cherubim,
A portion of the deep spiritual power
That pulses through the universe, and sways
Unmitigate the hearts of favored men;
So in this tempest I may bear me well,
And pass a stranger in the house of fear.
Be not my sins remembered to my cost;
But think that I have trod the thorny path,
The precipice of duty with a zeal,
Not measured by thy purpose infinite,
But such as 'neath the purest sun of faith
Could grow in passion's field.

Enter WENONAH.

              A little more,
I must stand in the solemn court of death,
And all mine acts by thine impartial eye
Be judged. If I have plainly dealt with men;
If I thy sleeve of patience have not frayed
And ravelled out by violence and sin,

Let thy strong arm support me in this stress;
Let thy good cheer be with me to the end.
    Totatomet.   A truce to this delay!
Pile on the fagots: let the dance begin!
    Wenonah. False Seconet! commend thy furiate
        soul
To the pure patience!—Braves, rest ye awhile!—
Pometacom, wake from this demon dream,
And snatch thy mercy from the gulf of blood
Where it is drowned. If ever I have done
Service to thee, give order to thy braves
To cut the withes that do the pale-face bind,
And set him free.
    Philip.   Thou ravest, Squaw.—
Take her away!
    Annawan.   Come! come!
In realm of old Pokanoket
We do not know command.
    Wenonah.   Unhand me, Chief!
And in this mood cross not my path.
    Annawan. Nay, here thou must weed out
That vice of temper, and obey.
    Wenonah. Thou gray iniquity! it is thy hand
That leads his purpose to this horror's verge.—
Sachem, a Seconet appeals to thee,
Head of a tribe that ever smoked with thine
The calumet of peace.
    Philip.   Didst thou not in thy lodge
Sit still, and send my braves away?
    Wenonah.   Pometacom,
It tortures me to see that stony look
Where no hope dwells.

Totatomet. Beware, Sachem, she hath a tongue
Crooked as the prone snake's.
 Wenonah. Wrap him not up
Within thy favor's cloak, for he hath sworn
Against my life. Sachem, lend me thine ear :
If I have ever harbored in my mind
Friendship or fear for aught in Plymouth sails,
I scuttle it in waters of my hate.
Five hundred braves whose ears the music drink
Of ocean's waves that foam on Sogkonate,
Shall hear with thee a sterner music breathe.
A coat of wampum will I weave for thee,
Whose price shall buy an hundred stand of arms ;
And I will pray the perfect one above
To hold thee in his hand, and victory drop
Forever on thy path.
 Philip. When I have set my foot
On all mine enemies, she offers this !—
Will ye not light the fire ?
 Wenonah. Hold ye !—Take all I have,
And grant me only this. Pometacom,
I turn me from thy soul in fury mired,
And pawing vainly up the bank of truth,
Unto thy nobler self in reason's chair
Seated, and made the guest of mercy. Chief,
Thy heart hath known the painful joy of love ;
Counted hast thou the minutes to the time
When thy fond eyes should mirror back the light
Which in ethereal beauty seemed a part
Of that pure sky that hangs above our heads :
Each minute shackled with the chain and ball
Of hours ; each hour slow pacing to his end
As if he bore upon his back a day.

Call up the ghosts of those departed days;
Call from the grave of time those dear delights;
And they shall plead for me with thunder tongues;
And in the race unto thy favor's goal,
Outstrip my words unwinged by eloquence,
As nimble deer outstrip the slow-paced bear.
Turn not thy face away! Here bends a knee
Which never yet the lowly earth hath kissed
In supplication; but sachems to it
Have bowed, and deemed their dignity increased:
Here do I kneel, and with my suitor breath
Laden with rich devotion to thy cause,
His freedom buy.
   Philip. Arise! I wonder thou shouldst plant
      thy love
Within a soul that hates thy native race.
   Wenonah. Let him who never owned the house
      of flame
Where dwells the human heart, my action blame.
   Philip.   I am resolved.
   Wenonah. Nay, Sachem, here I stay till thou
      dost turn
Thy passion out of doors, and graces peep,
Like cherubs, from thine eyes.
   Philip.   Plead not for him!
His life stood in his clutch if he renounce
The service of the English arms, and line
His fortune's cloak with honors of our race:
He trod upon the bosom of this chance,
As who should say, freedom and ampler breath
Grew nobler in the sunless fields of death.
   Wenonah.   Give to my love
What he denies to pride.

Philip.   No!
I am not one whose perfect plans are pushed
And jostled from their path by woman's whim ;
Nor would I bind an honor on my brow
But what is harvested in fields of war:
I shall not change.
    Wenonah.   Is every feeling of thy breast
Mortgaged to hardness? Power, I deem, should
        dwell
In lodge of clemency, no hand stretch forth
To nature's tyranny. Plucked is thy fame
From tree of terror ; it will shrivel up
And moulder on thy tomb : but let thy thoughts
Soar to the heaven of mercy, thou art indeed
The first man of the age.
    Philip.   Wenonah, I have said.
There is no inch of softness in my breast
For mercy's roots to grow : my warriors slain,
Their squaws and children banished in the sea,
Would rise with shadowy hands and cut it down.
Pity is fled from earth, and in the clouds
Maketh her home with spirits of the dead.
    Wenonah. Where am I ? Are those stars whose
        tranquil eyes
Should pity me, not mock my great despair ?
Are those the beings of my flesh and blood
Who should thrust in between my woe and thee,
A guard of love ? Like figures carved in rock
They stand, with lightnings wreathed around their
        brow.
Ye worse than wolves that not devour their own !
Had I the braves I vainly offered thee,
I had commanded, and ye would obey.

Pometacom, thou art dressed in fierce blood—
Blood spouting from thine eyes, thine ears and
  mouth,
And in hot currents flowing to the ground,
And leaping up in columns to thy head,
And surging like a sea in dull eclipse,
Till thou art all one crimson wave. Away!
To liberty my hand will carve thy way.

[*Dashes through the crowd to the stake, and cuts the
  thongs which bind the prisoner.*]

    Totatomet.   The witch
Loosens his bands—he's free!
    Wenonah. Take thou this knife—I have another
  here.
Flee! I will follow.
    Church. Make way! A death or two hangs in
  this blade.
I have new strength, and he who bars my way
Petitions death. Wenonah, leave me now.
    Wenonah. Nay, I will go.
Be quick, or they surround thee.
    Totatomet.   Thy fortune at the stake
Laughs, but—   [*Hurls his tomahawk.*
    Philip.   A nerveless arm!
Ho! seize him, braves!
    Church. For love of me, Wenonah, leave the
  fray.
Philip must pardon thee. If I escape—

[*Warwhoops resound on all sides, and the Indians rush
to seize* CHURCH, *who strikes down several and turns
to flee.*]

Totatomet. What! doth he go?
Furies that ride the scorching blasts of hell
Fondle this hand! [*Stabs* WENONAH.
Wenonah. Thou spotted heart! The ashes of
remorse
Strangle thy prayers!—Fly, Church, and live!
Church. I curse me that I live till now.
Lighter than air, yet heavier far than fate,
Rest on my heart, and in its chamber dark
Thy perfect soul shall sit and rule my thoughts
Till death befriends me too. I cannot go,
And see thee nevermore.—Who follows, dies!

[*Takes up* WENONAH *in his arms, and disappears in the forest.*]

Annawan. Foiled by a squaw!
Philip. Let five or six the fleetest braves pursue,
And bring him back, alive or dead.—
[*Exeunt several braves.*
The Ruler pardon thee, Totatomet;
For thou hast broke her beauteous vase of life,
And shook the perfume of its mortal flower
Rudely in air. I loved thee as a son;
But henceforth be no warrior of mine.
Totatomet. Sachem,
I have shook hands with desperation; so
I bow me to thy will, and from thy tree
Bark my dear hopes, how dear I cannot tell.
But first I exile from my use this knife
Which hath trod in her side, as cursed thing;
For it would scorch my hand and burn withal
The marrow of my bones, in thought of her:

But ye the precious drops that stain its lips,
I will entreasure.
   [*Dries the knife on his breast, and throws it down.*
I pray thee, thine: something I have to do.
                              [*To* AGAMAUG.
Farewell, Pometacom! Her did I love;
But love's sweet dew in fang of jealousy
Sucked and distilled, to poisonous frenzy turns.
The pale-face lives; and for his trail and mine
Too narrow is the earth.   [*Exit.*
   Philip.   On the air their voices die!
Ere the night wind unbinds that lace of cloud
From the moon's neck, they will be back; and then
No accident can set denial's foot
On thy great hope.
   Annawan.   I am not sure: with hosts of fiends
He is in league. Hearing he is at large
Will sadden me. Ho! double the pursuit!
A belt of wampum in my wigwam hangs
For him who brings his scalp.
                       [*Exeunt several braves.*
   Philip.   I clothed me in a robe
With all our battles painted in bright hues,
And there his burning death. If he surprise
Freedom, my fortune now at fullest orb
Begins to wane.   [*Exeunt.*

SCENE III.—THE FOREST IN POKANOKET. An Indian
trail crossing a deep glen which opens on the sea.
Night: as the scene progresses the day dawns.

  Enter CHURCH *bearing* WENONAH.

 Church. This point of woods laying an ebon
  hand
Slim on the white cheek of the sovereign sea,
Should be the south coast of Pokanoket.
No further can I go; my walls of strength
Surrender to exhaustion. If no aid
Come with the dawn, that light rebukes and ends
These saucy woes, to me the truest aid.
My precious burden here will I lay down
On this green bed spread by the gracious sun.
Dead! dead! Fair casket of the richest soul
Ever was current in this sordid world,
With its pure coin to buy my worthless life.
But see! with stealthy pace the blood creeps back
In her cold cheek, hoisting his standard there
To rally hope.
 Wenonah. Ah me!
 Church.   Wenonah!
 Wenonah.   Are we still pursued?
 Church.   The darkness puts to sleep
Their drowsy chase.
 Wenonah.   Blood has been shed,
And thou art wounded too.
 Church.   Had some knife
Gifted my body with a mortal blow,
I now were happy.
 Wenonah.   Thou shouldst have left

Me to my fate, and put thine own true life
Beyond their reach. How are we here?
    Church.   It will distress thee more:
Think not of it.
    Wenonah.   Nay, the story I will take,
Token of thee, to that home the west wind
Is winging me, and treasure it for aye.
    Church.   Two I had slain; one held the trail
Outstripping his dull comrades in the race,
And chid my yawning speed till further flight
No glimpse of safety saw. I turned me round:
With swifter spring leaps not the incensed bear
When in a bone-strewn cave, lit by her eyes,
A hunter seeks her cubs, than at his throat
I flew, his yell entombing ere its birth;
And feasted in his blood my hungry knife.
The end is not yet: another must drain
That fatal chalice, hostage still for thee.
    Wenonah.   I die content.
Look on me so! Within thy glance I see
A speechless tongue that doth translate thy love
In language of devotion that knows not
The dialect of change. This timeless end
Trips up the retinue of golden days
My fancy started when our lives as one
Should drift to God on waves of happiness;
And when thy hand should loose my virgin zone,
And me make mother of some old-time race
To plant an iron age. The sword of fate
Thrust from the ambush of a friendly hand,
Remorseless falls, and mutilates my hope:
But how I love thee!
    Church.   This is more cruel loss

To plough and harrow o'er my brow of life,
Than all the fiery dangers I have passed.
Had I been tutored in the stoic creed,
I'd throw away the gift of longer days
To follow thee—friends, honor, and the fame
That lackeys deeds of praise, all, all that earth
Holds dear, and view them motes in thy great beam
Of rapture-giving thoughts. A radiant one,
Hallowed and perfect, will I hold thee here,
Till time in pity cuts my mortal thread.

Wenonah. Come nearer, Church! I wish to feel
    thine arm
Around me—there is stealing over me
An icy breath—and cold invades my limbs—
And feelings strange do harbor in my heart.
A calmness as of sleep creeps to my brain,
And rings my senses in a sisterhood
Of dreams. Like lappings of the ocean's tongue
On face of a pebbled strand, the sounds of earth
Are smothered in mine ear. Remember me—
And think I only loved my life for thee. [*Dies.*

Enter TOTATOMET.

Church. Farewell, forever fare thee well!
Now heaven lead me half the height she scaled,
And I am worthy!—Ha! thou damned wretch!
My tongue it blisters to articulate
Thy hell-born name.

Totatomet. Thou canst not loathe it more than I.

Church. What wouldst thou here,
Thou mailed in guiltiness? Hast come to gloat
Over my misery, and to steep thy hate
Up to its very top in horror's gulf?

Behold the tragic burden of this earth!
Look where thy knife staggered in her dear side,
And churlishly thrust to the vulgar air
The fairest soul that in a house of clay
Did ever dwell. Thee shall damnation seize,
And drag thee down the howling coast of hell,
Where fiends shall fly with thee in burning winds,
Or swim through lakes of sulphur, and all time
Griddle thy flesh on endless coals of fire,
As I could now.

   Totatomet.   Thy passion shall not wring
Out of my cold despair a single word.
Stand thou aside awhile; for I would plant
In my sad mind the tokens of a face
Whose beauty I did worship. It is our trait
The red man never weeps; else could mine eyes
Pour drops as fast as bearded spruce their gum
On the black ground, when spring unchains its life;
Washing in love those pure and livid lines,
Till tears had thawed the icy hand of death.—
Strew ashes on your heads, ye Seconets!
And wail in shrillest voice; for she is dead
Whose sway poured honor on our Sogkonate.
This hand was traitor to my purposes,
That should in loyal service of thy life
Grow lean and wrinkled, rather than betray.
I had not thought in this to play the squaw;
Nor deemed that in the valleys of my heart
The flowers of pity grew. If curses come,
My soul will bow and bid them welcome: meet
It is that I should suffer. Fare thee well!—
Pale-face, what wouldst thou have!

   Church.   Naught but thy life.

Totatomet.   A foeman dost thou see not greatly
         cares
If victory shall on his banner perch.
I stand within the ruins of my life :
Ever the same to me is peace or strife.
The Seconet is ready.
   Church.   Then to it.
   [*They fight with knives :* TOTATOMET *falls.*]
   Totatomet.   Pale-face,
I thank thee, though thy hand did strike in hate.
With us it is a crime to slay the chief
Who in our tribal lodges bears a sway :
An exile he must be, and every hand
Devoted to his death.   Me hast thou freed
By strumpet chance ensnared, and in the air
Of nobler fortunes set.   [*Dies.*
   Church.   I am undone ; this triumph costs me
        dear :
It cannot balm my deep and gaping wounds.
Thy life for hers thrown in the scale of fate
Is light as down ; and mine is desolate,
Hope-barren as the deeds this night hath seen.
The burning lips of fever suck my wounds ;
Upon my shoulders hangs a robe of fire :
This dell is like to be a triple grave.
Come, dissolution, with thy fingers cold
And close my door of sense ; and all the lights
Of hope and pride that in this mansion burn
Snuff out : let valor die that had no power
To snatch her from the frosty kiss of death ;
Be hatred rampant on this earthly stage,
And slaughter raging here with crimson jaws

Dig ancient chaos from the grave of time ;
Eclipse tear from the forehead of the sky
The golden tresses of the hateful sun ;
And the vast night preach in his pulpit black
The sermon of the dead.   [*Falls in a swoon.*

   Enter SAMPONCUT.

Samponcut. By Segwun's tears !
I little thought to find me here—ah me !
But who can stand the siege of scolding wife?
All day she did bombard my ears with cries
And wailings for her " Squaw," her " motherling,"
Her "sweet Wenonah," till my temples throbbed
Like pines in the fierce blasts of winter's wind.
My meat was sauced with her reproaches loud ;
The glass of my sweet sleep was cracked by them.
What could I do ? I like an easy time
Loafing around the village, and to snooze
Under an oak the long, long summer day ;
Or to lie fishing on a grassy bank
As moveless as a turbid rattlesnake
Clutched by the frost down in his stony den.
But, by the hoary beard of Peboan !
My peace was taken captive by her tongue ;
And nothing could it ransom back again
But I should go and find the Sachemess,
And bring her home.
I bade adieu to all my ancient haunts ;
And stored my bark with clams and venison,
In loyal homage to my belly's lord ;
For many plans are marred that to this god
Neglect to sacrifice : and as the sun
Stood tip-toe on the blue Pocasset hills,

I girded up my loins, and wended on.
Ugh! If I be not shot in wanton blood
By some of those young bucks from Plymouth
    town,
And scalped alive, a seventh son am I,
And snap my lucky fingers at mischance.
But now the infant day in cloudy locks
Is peering out the windows of the east,
And I must spur my jaded valor on.
But soft! What have we here? A sleeping brave?
Rouse, sluggard, rouse! Too precious are these
    hours
To gird the waist of slumber! Art thou drunk?
As I do live it is Totatomet.
What ho! Totatomet! No moving yet!
He's soaked in blood, and hears no earthly call.
Ha! what is this beyond? A ghastly crop
This dingle bears. A squaw! Our Seconet!
Oh death! thou harvestest the ripe and the unripe;
And crammest full thy barns with human grain,
To glut thy winter maw! Who groaneth there?
Is one alive?

    Church.   Help!
    Samponcut.   Hist!
    Church.   Help! if thou hast a heart
That beats for human woe.
    Samponcut.   I know that voice.
    Church. Thou art a Seconet, and hadst the part
Of service in her life who lies in coldness.
Bind up my wounds that fester in the air;
And have my thanks and the report of deeds
To slake thy wonder's thirst.
    Samponcut.   I will do so;

And pray thy hand is free of such black guilt
In tearing down and robbing of its light
That beauteous house. So, so : now canst thou
    stand ?
I'll lead thee to my boat in yonder cove :
And then return to ship this dismal freight,
And steer us home.
  Church. [*Kneels at Wenonah's side.*]
            Let me but coffin in mine arms
This dear mortality. The birds awake,
And cradle in the air their happy songs ;
But we shall never hear thy voice again.
Thy beauty is bequeathed to miser death
Whose halls are crowded with the lovely ones
Of this sad earth, and still unsatisfied
Drafts us for more.—
            Bear with me, Seconet ;
For this subdues my fortitude. No more !
Lead on ! I've felt my sorrows as a man :
Now bend my looks the future's brow to scan.
                              [*Scene closes.*

ACT V.

SCENE I.—PLYMOUTH. *The shore of the Bay, with Plymouth Rock: the ground covered with snow.*

Enter a Citizen.

Citizen. In Thy sight a thousand years
Are but as yesterday, and as a watch
Upon the hills of night. How even now
Thine anger doth consume us, and Thy wrath
Makes us afraid.

Enter Second Citizen.

Hast heard the rumor, Job?
Second Citizen. Now, by my faith!
Mine ears are stuffed with rumors, as an inn
On snowy night with belated travellers.
First Citizen. But this one smacks of truth, and it will slap
The face of thy composure. It is said
The army is defeated and dispersed—
That goodly force bearing in its strong hand
Our best, last hope. Alack! we are undone.
Second Citizen. Fie on that garrulous dame!
Truth hang her up in chains, and then cut out
Her thousand tongues. But Church our master leads;
And when he steers the vessel of the war,
I sleep in peace.

First Citizen. I fear me for that noble band
Whose steps are meshed in snows, while icy winds
Fold them in death. So long hath victory's arms
Fondled the name of Philip, we but live
In suburbs of her love.
   Second Citizen.   Nay, Humble Ames,
Quell thy despair and pin thy faith to Church.
He studied in the school of Indian arts:
Each trick of ambush, manner of attack
He is familiar with. If any one
Can coax a smile from lips of stern mischance,
Church is the man.—

      Enter a MESSENGER.

     Golightly, art thou from the camp?
  Messenger.   Ay, Master Job.
  Second Citizen. Well, what's the word?
  Messenger.   Too feeble is my breath
To lift the news to hearing.
  First Citizen.   'Tis heavy then?
I never knew a one who bore good news
But blurts it out.
  Messenger. Ha! ha! ha! If my speed had not
The last two hours devoured a dozen miles,
I would be merry.
  First Citizen. I would thy legs might teach thy
     tongue
Some better speed.
  Second Citizen. Come! come! tell us the worst.
  Messenger. Ye drooping hearts! from garden of
     your mind
Weed out that thought. If hundreds of the red
Devils with bloody arms their bride of death

ACT V.

SCENE I.—PLYMOUTH. The shore of the Bay, with Plymouth Rock: the ground covered with snow.

Enter a CITIZEN.

Citizen. In Thy sight a thousand years
Are but as yesterday, and as a watch
Upon the hills of night. How even now
Thine anger doth consume us, and Thy wrath
Makes us afraid.

Enter SECOND CITIZEN.

Hast heard the rumor, Job?
Second Citizen. Now, by my faith!
Mine ears are stuffed with rumors, as an inn
On stormy night with lated travellers.
First Citizen. But this one smacks of truth, and it will slap
The face of thy composure. It is said
The army is defeated and dispersed—
That goodly force bearing in its strong hand
Our best, last hope. Alack! we are undone.
Second Citizen. Fie on that garrulous dame!
Truth hang her up in chains, and then cut out
Her thousand tongues. Ben Church our muster leads;
And when he steers the vessel of the war,
I sleep in peace.

First Citizen. I fear me for that noble band
Whose steps are meshed in snows, while icy winds
Fold them in death. So long hath victory's arms
Fondled the name of Philip, we but live
In suburbs of her love.
  Second Citizen.   Nay, Humble Ames,
Quell thy despair and pin thy faith to Church.
He studied in the school of Indian arts :
Each trick of ambush, manner of attack
He is familiar with. If any one
Can coax a smile from lips of stern mischance,
Church is the man.—

Enter a MESSENGER.

            Golightly, art thou from the camp ?
  Messenger.   Ay, Master Job.
  Second Citizen. Well, what's the word ?
  Messenger.   Too feeble is my breath
To lift the news to hearing.
  First Citizen.   'Tis heavy then ?
I never knew a one who bore good news
But blurts it out.
  Messenger. Ha! ha! ha! If my speed had not
The last two hours devoured a dozen miles,
I would be merry.
  First Citizen. I would thy legs might teach thy
    tongue
Some better speed.
  Second Citizen. Come ! come ! tell us the worst.
  Messenger. Ye drooping hearts! from garden of
    your mind
Weed out that thought. If hundreds of the red
Devils with bloody arms their bride of death

Clasping, charred in the flames that wrapped their
    fort
In robes of ruin, seem to you a loss,
What, then, is victory?
   First Citizen. How now! what dost thou say?
   Second Citizen. Ho! give him time, and he will
    weave
A glorious tale.
   Messenger. Rather put in my clutch
That dark green bottle, and my tongue will run
Fast as thy wish.
   Second Citizen. Odds boddikins! my manners
    slept.   [*Gives him a flask.*
   Messenger. Silence itself will this make elo-
    quent.   [*Drinks.*
Know, then, our arms have kissed the mouth of
    triumph;
And in the Narraganset swamp have backward
    rolled
The tide of Indian conquest. 'Twas a day
That did make faces at our bodily ease;
In which the elements struggled with man
For first degree and prize of cruelty.
With swords of snow and sleet the surly air
Guarded the pathway to the hostile town:
So little day could elbow through the storm
We deemed that jealous night usurped his throne.
Besides high palisades, hedges of trees
A rod in thickness, felled around the fort,
Our valor mocked and dressed our hopes in black.
No way was there to enter but a log
Spanning the moat, which passage did forbid
To more than one.

With courage that in golden letters writ
Should be bound in the deathless book of fame,
Our faithful soldiers trod that faithless path
Where death's vast tongue did lick them up by
    scores.
In deadly silence was their place supplied;
And still those borrowed lives were ravined down
The throats of flame. And all indeed was lost,
But that a desperate band by Mosely led,
Taught to unhoard their blood at freedom's call,
And shrug at death the shoulder of contempt,
Had got them in the rearward of the fort.
These, hand to hand, contended with the braves
At fearful odds, until the cry "They run,"
Larded their ribs of fright with such fresh force,
It struck a panic in the Indian host.
Then was the hand of terror wide unclasped;
And slaughter like a fiend broken from hell
Did stride amid their ranks. From lodge to lodge
In anguish flying, pappooses, squaws, and braves
Our swords pursued, and supped them in their
    blood.
In heaps on heaps, a weltering mass they lay,
The ruby currents of their ebbing hearts
The banks of snow dissolving. Give me grace,
If our revenge did shock the marble face
Of heaven; for in our breasts did Ate dwell,
And, shrieking, gentle mercy bade farewell.
Now yield me food and rest.
    Second Citizen.   Thou shalt have all.
The wonder and contentment in my breast
So strive, my tongue is conscript to the war,
And looks must do his office. This will be

To Winslow's mind the shadow of a great rock
Within a weary land. Pray he return!
Go thou, good Humble, and apprise the town
With chimes and ringing of the merry bells
In the embattled church,
That fortune now to us is penitent,
And hath no thought but to our vantage bent.
   First Citizen. I will; and soon your company will join
To hear Golightly once again recoin
His wondrous tale.
   Second Citizen.   Do so, and be
Welcome.—Come, Malachi!   [*Exeunt.*

SCENE II. THE FOREST IN POCASSET. An Indian form flits between the trees, followed presently by others, in twos and threes. Then solitude, broken only by the tap of a woodpecker on the trunk of a white pine.

AGAMAUG, ensconced in a clump of scrub oak, glides like a snake over the scene, and peers down the aisles of trees. Satisfied, apparently, there are no foes, he rises to his feet, and utters a guttural "Onaway." The screen of columbine which covers the mouth of a cave in the rocks is parted, and ALDERMAN with noiseless tread stands at his brother's side.

   Agamaug.   Their footsteps wander from the trail,
And danger us no more. Our greatest foe
Sits at our council fire.

Alderman.   Come, Agamaug, no more of that.
Agamaug.   The mama studs the trunk of yonder
   pine
With wormy acorns, so its famine dies
When snow the ground besieges.   Shall we less?
   Alderman.   The pelican will dip her bill
In her own heart, to feed her fainting young.
Into the chasm of our nation's need
Should we not throw our lives?
   Agamaug.   But answer me:
Are our free souls in bondage to his will,
And may not drink the air of their resolves?
   Alderman.   Let never echo chase those words
      again,
For they do blur thy gloss of loyalty ;
And in their action and report will pull
Misfortune on thy life.   Brother, be calm !
   Agamaug.   Is the sea calm when the rough winds
Tear out its crystal hair, and dash it down
On the grim rocks ?   Nay, teach Pometacom
A gentle way.
   Alderman.   Will the pine stoop
Its shoulder to the brake, the eagle nest
Beside the wren?
   Agamaug.   We should not to his desperate pur-
      pose dye
Our own clear minds ; nor dip his mad designs
In fountain of our praise.   The Chiefs are in revolt,
And grasp this sad occasion by the hand
To save the remnant of their broken tribes.
In mournful tones the Swamp defeat doth tell
Pokanoket to freedom bids farewell.
   Alderman.   It may be so, but in his fame I have

A lover's privilege, and now I am
Alone with him.
    Agamaug.   How! What says he?
    Alderman.   When my will was law,
The torch of victory was passed along
From hand to hand of battle, till it grew
One canopy of fire that dropped on earth
Embers of massacre whose hundred throats
Sucked up the English power.
    Agamaug.   His opportunity,
Not seized at proper time, is ever gone.
A thousand hearts whose golden blood did pass
In deeds of terror o'er the shrieking land,
Lie shrouded in the clotted slime and ooze
That creeps in silence round that fatal fort:
No voice may call them from the mortal sleep
In which ambition's hand hath buried them.
And is his genius so omnipotent
That it can clothe the beings of his brain
With flesh and blood, to rush into the gap
Mown by his pride, and to the whites present
An undejected brow?
    Alderman.   Call it no fault of his if treason's hand
Unlatched our hope in Narraganset Swamp.
Already hath he bandaged up that loss
On field of Lancaster; and to the whites
Marching in Medfield held
The goblet of defeat.
The Sachem's fortune, one foot in the grave,
Pulls not his courage after. He desponds
Never, nor bends the head of confidence
To knee of doubt; for doubts are foxes' breed,
And do betray us in the hour of need.

Agamaug.   Wah !
With flattery his deeds are fenced around ;
And there be none with soul enough to dare
Let down the bars of censure.
    Alderman.   Agamaug,
For that he woke the giant of this strife
In noble cause, his race will cherish him ;
And any word that purpose doth deny
Grows in the swamp of malice. Let us die,
And fill one common grave, than now draw back,
And stoop to lick that wronging hand.
    Agamaug.   Nay, rather let us live,
And work our mission out. A timely peace
Which we may mould in likeness of our wish,
With arms in hand ; a portion of our lands ;
The lives we bear and those we hold in love ;
And silent memories of heroic deeds,
May purchase now. I go to the dread Chief,
Bearing this bitter draught ; and I will sing
Even unto his face the tragic note
That in my ear is ringing.
    Alderman. Alas ! thou knowest not Pometacom
If thou dost think his soul will kneel to peace
While loyalty can marshal to the fray
A single spirit of Pokanoket ;
While his right arm the listening air can charm
With music of the whizzing tomahawk.
I love thee, Agamaug, and would not see
Thy life stand in the lightning of his wrath.
    Agamaug. His sway is but the child of our
        desires,
And not their master. Fare thee well !

Alderman.   Unhappy man! I fear me for the worst
While this resentment spurs thy foaming thoughts
To brink of danger.   I will go with thee.

                                                    [*Exeunt.*

SCENE III.   METAPOISET.   The Indian camp on the banks of the Taunton.

        Enter PHILIP *and* TATOSON.

Tatoson.   By the skin
Of the fierce rattlesnake twined in my hair,
The totem which I worship, it is true :
Their loose allegiance have the Pecomptucks
Thrown off, and scattered to their river towns.
  Philip.   False as water, fickle as the wind !
They were the last to dig the hatchet up,
The first to bury it.   Time-servers' minds
The cord of faith and honor never binds.—

        Enter ANNAWAN.

What mutiny now walks abroad ?
  Annawan.   Pometacom,
Throw not on me that eye of basilisk
That kills with looking.
  Philip.   Be content :
I hurt them not I love.
  Annawan.   Hear, then !   The Nipmuck chief,
Clasping the hand of rude rebellion, hath
Called all his braves from the projected fray,
And sullenly files back his homeward way.
  Philip.   Thou art a man so perfect and complete,
It ill becomes thy parts to father lies.

Let tongues that never warned, though they should be
Organs of nature or the sky's rapt tones,
Knock at my door of hearing with those words,
I should but cram them down their joyless throats,
Saying they lie.
    Annawan. My Chief, 'tis even so;
And that it's so, I grieve me I had eyes
To draw the image of that basest act
Upon my sense recoiling.
    Philip.   Traitors!
If there be any word of deeper shame
To soak their memory in and rot their name,
I want it now.
    Annawan. There is more;
But none have dared to bring the news to thee,
And I will strangle the misshapen birth
Even in bed of utterance.
    Philip.   Nay, go on:
I am a rock where fiercest surge of grief
May beat in vain.
    Annawan.   Dear Sachem,
nfected by the virus of revolt,
Deeming the issue travels to despair,
The Narragansets have drawn off their bands
And fasten on the moccasin of peace.
    Philip. I pray you, look,
And tell me if I seem a common man
Whose eye hath lost its sway. If I am less,
This fadeless cause should dilate in their thought
To mountain size, and dwarf all earthly things.
Oh reputation! art thou but a cloak
That one may turn or cast away at will,

Even as suits his whim, and buy from time
Trappings of approbation that will blind
The eyes of men to rottenness within !
My fortunes are corrupted by the blood
That should ennourish them. Why do I chide?
Let treason come ! I did not beckon it ;
I held me clear. If they with most foul hands
Deflower our mission's virgin purity,
I have respected it and held it dear.—

    Enter TUSPAQUIN.

Now, Assawomset, choke these venom throats,
Or play a cheerful strain.
 Tuspaquin. Pometacom, my Chief,
In cabin of thy fortune I have lodged ;
And I will be a neighbor to thy loss.
 Philip. If we have read our wampum right,
Thine is a race steadfast to its resolves.
It medicines the sickness of my state
To look on thee : I know that thou hast played
Well thy last part.
 Tuspaquin. Sachem, some other tongue must be
The deputy of what I bear.
 Philip. Ha ! what is it ? Speak out !
I am so deep in sorrow's bitter sea
Nothing can push me further.
 Tuspaquin. Good my Chief,
What they have told thee of desertions base,
Of that rebellious tide upon thy shore
Creeping with inky feet, and battles lost,
Are but the prologue to this greater scene
Writ out by pen of shame.

Philip. Well!
Thou seest me how I stand.
   Tuspaquin. At Acushnet
With all the Assawomset braves I lay,
Guarding thy squaw and child confided us
In hope we might grope through the cloud of
    whites,
And in the bleak north an asylum find
Kinder than men. The fingers of the dawn
Had just unlaced the purple robe of night,
When led by Church a hundred Plymouth men,
Like lightning swords flashing from vapor sheaths,
Fell on us sleeping. Musket voices belched
Their leaden missives folded up in flame,
That argued down the whooping of my braves.
Our angry guns answered the challenge stern,
Giving to death a legacy of foes.
With mine own arm three did I cleave to earth,
But two to one they overmatched our strength;
And valor made a flatterer of retreat.
We fled: I sought Oneka and thy son;
But in the surge of battle they were borne
On rocks of bondage. Sachem, I am unfit
Longer to breathe the beneficial air:
Take thou this blade and sheathe it in my breast.

[*Kneels before* PHILIP, *bares his bosom, and offers him his knife.*]

   Philip. A many perils have I passed, but this
Staggers my mind. Is it so, Annawan?
I look upon the ground, and yet it yawns
No bottomless mouth to draw me in. The heavens
That once were fair and noble to my sight,

Now seem more terrible than serpents' eyes
When they strike them in men's to fascinate.
I had a heart within whose gates did pass
A regiment of tender sentiments;
But it hath grown to marble in this hour.
   Annawan. Thy words have drifted on his heart
A bitter snow. Better, away.
   Tuspaquin.   I'll find a ditch,
And there my body lay.   [*Exit.*
   Philip.   Where hath he gone?
Bear with me, braves, if I a gentle thought
Bequeath to those perfections. It is past;
And now I turn me from that black abyss
Where all that smoothed the hardness of my life,
And featured me, is clasped in arms of loss;
And buckle on the belt of fortitude,
This monster world defying.

      Enter AGAMAUG *and* ALDERMAN.

                        What bold dismay
Posts on your tongues? Strike on! I alter not
If cataracts of woe burst on my head,
So stony is it here.   [*Strikes his breast.*
   Alderman. What cause hast thou!
   Philip. Says any one that I
Have not done well? Or could my fortunes grow
Forever, like that reptile of the south
Mud-dwelling, when my instruments are men?
   Agamaug.   Pometacom,
The Manitou is angry with his sons,
And speaks his censure so.
   Annawan. Now, if my friendship yet

Is honored of thy mind, go kill such words
On thine own tongue.
    Philip. Great Medicine, wilt thou sew up
This ragged time?
    Agamaug.   Listen, Pometacom,
For in thy hand is held the doom of men.
The time is deathly sick; and to a grave
Hobble our pallid fortunes. We have played
The fatal game of war, and we have lost.
The allies have deserted; in our ranks
Treason and pestilence walk hand in hand,
And daily thin our sturdy ribs of war.
Like withered leaves we shudder in the blast
Of English power which, from the sea-bathed east,
Rushes with gloomy hands to strip our tree.
The flower of Pokanoket is in the earth;
And whispers in the dusty ear of death,
" We fell in vain!" The living be thy care;
And while we may with free and sovereign breath
Parley with fate for honorable terms,
Seize the occasion, and our country's wounds
Close up and heal.
    Alderman. Sachem, in the dim woods that nurse
Strange forms of thought, visions have come to him;
But if his counsel sits in lodge of harshness,
And grates upon thine ear, his purpose is
Attorney to our weal.
    Philip.   Have ye now done,
Or do ye hold in leash to slip on me
Fresh hounds of grief?
    Agamaug.   Sachem,
I voice the feeling of the tribe.
    Philip.   No!

Agamaug.   Yes!

Philip. How! all are recreant to their faith,
And kiss the haggard cheek of this revolt?
If this were true, I would push off
The mountain of my days, and the false tribe
Captain with thee. But no!
Thou sowest in mine ear
A slander. Now have done!

Alderman. No more of this! Come!

Agamaug. [*Going.*] Whom the Great Spirit
would destroy,
He first of reason robs.

Philip. Thou art a child: our safety lies
But in the victor arm.

Agamaug. [*Returning.*] Must all be sacrificed
To offer bloody incense to thy fame?
Loss piled on loss, defeat upon defeat,
Till war's hand build him of the red men's bones
A ghastly monument that shall outstare
The blazing eye of heaven, to after-times
Writing the folly of Pometacom.

Annawan. The serpent sings; the eagle flies:
My maiden love is in the skies.

Philip. Oh cold adversity! teach me restraint!

Alderman. Thy judgment slumbers: come!

Agamaug. I never bound my free thought to
control.—
Sachem, this is a time to shut the door
In face of flattery, and see ourselves,
Even as we do live, in glass of truth.
We dwelt beneath the genial sun of peace;
In numbers grew apace; and wrapped us up
In richest mantle of prosperity.

We were content; but still there crouched in thee
An evil spirit envious of our lot,
That fired thy soul to hottest lust of war,
And lured it blindly to adulterate
In gay ambition's bed. Oh, for a voice
Whose deep echoes might live in ear of time;
And at the mention of thine ill-starred name,
Start up and rave in solemn warning tones:
" Thou wert thy country's curse, and dropped disease
Upon her healthy state, and gave thy will
A free bridle to drive her to her ruin."

Philip. Hang at thy throat
The red fangs of the wolf, and strangle thee!
I sin against the freedom of my state
In wording this with thee. But for I wish
Thy passion should not smear the name I bear
Purely before these dear and veteran braves,
My vengeance should not lag behind mine ire,
But bathe it in thy blood. What! I?—
Ingrateful wretch, how many beads of favor
Dost thou unstring—
The blood I dropped on twenty glorious fields
Should rise to life, and stifle in thy throat
That giant lie. I gave the nation all;
And if fidelity may brag of one
That loved her with unspotted soul, 'tis he
Who stands within thy sleet of injury.
Away! and live! or I shall lay on thee
Hands that are terrible.

Agamaug. I go, but not from fear. Be thou
Still governed by thy dark and desperate will;
Quaff blood like water; be thy stepping-stones

Skulls which shall pave this lost Pokanoket
As stars the sky ; and set thee up a court
Only of the pale dead.
   Philip.   Where thou shalt reign !   [*Stabs him.*
   Alderman.   Who striketh him,
Doth make a foe of me.
   Annawan.   Make way !
Put up thy hatchet—so !   [*Disarms Alderman.*
   Philip.   Braves, treason's tooth had gnawn away
      the thongs
That bound his duty to Pokanoket ;
And so I struck lest he betray us too,
And face the garment of ingratitude
With blackest infamy.
   Alderman.   Pometacom, let that deep lie
Blister thy tongue !
   Philip.   Ha !
   Alderman.   Stand back !—
How is it, Agamaug ?
   Agamaug.   Thou must dwell in the evil days ;
But I am free. With kind hands to my grave
Bring me a gourd of water and fresh food,
That so my soul be armored from the fiends
On its last journey. It was the tribe's hope.
Whatever he says, innocent I die :
Prove it to men, thou witness in the sky !   [*Dies.*
   Alderman.   Farewell, thou noble heart !
I thought thy way to herald in the grave,
Not follow it. Peace to thy gentle shade ;
And all good spirits guard thee to the land
Happy with light of never-ending day.—
Pometacom, wrong hast thou done in this ;
And wakened here a feeling that will slake

Its bitter thirst at fountain of thy heart.
His face was dear to me; his little steps
I led when first a child he clung and played
Around our father's lodge. I taught his arm
To bend the ashen bow; and his quick cries
Of boyish joy when sped the mimic shaft,
Was music in mine ear. His golden dawn
Lighted the forehead of my manly prime:
In thought I lived my youth again in him.
He camped within my love; he was the eye
With which I saw the world, and thought it fair;
And as we ranged beneath the hoary trees,
The gracious silence seemed to subtly weave
In one firm thread the feelings of our hearts.
In slaying him thou hast slain part of me;
And poisoned at its source the loyalty
I bore thy person and devoted cause.
Revolt and deadly hate are now my liege;
And they do cut away and amputate
My gangrened worship. In the tides of war
That lap thy feet, mine arm will swim the first;
And rising on a cloud of vengeance up
To spleen my sky of rage, at last shall fall
A thunderbolt on thee.   *[Exit.*
  Philip. Through misery's wide thicket leads
My way of life: forever must I live
Vassal to fear, though ye, I think, are true.
It was a golden mouth, and would have stirred
Against our arms some quick and nimble wrong.
He tempted fate, and on forbearance' back
Put such a load, my justice threw it off.
Give him such burial as befits a brave;
Then meet me in the gulch where lies a band

Posted to intercept the whites. The scouts
Must soon return with fresh intelligence.
This ambush will reset our broken fight,
And give the traitors pause. Away! [*Exeunt.*

SCENE IV.—POKANOKET. The English camp on the edge of a swamp. Night: the camp-fires burning. Soldiers bivouacked under the trees.

Enter CHURCH *and* GOLDING.

Golding. He reports
The remnant of the thinned Wampanoags
Have mustered their despair in yonder swamp,
To make a last appeal to victory.
Church. It is but trial of their heels again,
Or battle on our terms.
Golding. They will run,
For these defeats pour in their willing ears
The sweetness of their former life of peace.
Desertions are as frequent as the bright
Visits the cheerful dawn pays to the east:
The few that drop their sad-eyed, stone-cold hopes
Into the ocean of fidelity,
Quickly will seize the hand of any chance
That leads to door of peace.
Church. True, Philip's strong will alone
Cements the wall of their resistance: he
Taken or dead, their edifice of war
Will crumble down.
Golding. My Captain, this campaign
Powders thy sky with honors, and thy name

Brevets with ne plus ultra ; but the thought
Roots not the sorrow from thy countenance
Some loss hath planted there. Yet I have heard
Men will in solemn moments of their lives,
As this is now, a premonition feel
Of death's sad coming, when they see beyond
Horizons of the present to the day
Presiding over our mortality.
  Church.   Ah, Golding,
There is no magic in the morrow's fray
To spell my spirits into banishment.
I go to it with such a willing mind
As he may hold who seeks his bridal couch ;
Or any careless heart that casts its sail
On fortune's waves, and sees in fancy ride
A golden shore whose sands shall wash his hope
With riches of Peru. But this difference mine :
While they set in their view the happy end,
As love, possessions, quest of noble deeds,
I value them as nothing more than dross,
And consecrate and crown the labor's brow
But with the joy of doing.
  Golding.   Some poisoned shaft
Hath drunk the fountain of thy genial ways,
Where we have seen the figure of a wish
To walk the world in plausive voice of men.
  Church. Ay, thou dost touch
That frail desire with finger of the truth,
Which now is but an echo in my life,
The skeleton of all my sturdy hopes.
How my ambition's stream out of its course
Rudely was turned by fate's malignant hand,
And creeps in dull bed of " I-do-not-care,"

Thy sympathy shall know.
I wooed an Indian maiden; and my love
Was of so high and regal quality,
It ordered from their place all meaner things
That stand and cry " deliver," to the world.
My passion found a kingdom in her soul
Where every waking thought a courtier was
That knelt in duty at my throne of love.
Our vows were plighted, and we but delayed
A holy sanction till this vase of war
Was cracked to pieces by the hand of peace.
In Hadley fight where Lothrop's regiment
Sank in the mire of slaughter, with his life,
I fell a captive to Totatomet,
A brave of Sogkonate; and by command
Of Philip was I sentenced to the stake.
The brush and fagots round my feet were piled;
The swarthy faces of the jeering braves
Shot glances 'thwart the lurid pine-knot fires,
That gave a foretaste of the horrid draught
Distilled for me; and plunged an icy hand
Deep in my blood.

Golding.   It would have laid in fear
An iron heart.

Church. I stood that moment on the edge of life.
An hour's flight, and 'mid the warriors' yells,
Ferried on burning wings of agony,
My spirit must have sped in that black gulf
That bounds these mortal shores. And fabling hope
Which is our nurse of life, deserted me;
And I, a truant from the perfect faith,
In mine extremity had put my thoughts

Grown up in sin, to school of our great Master,
That haply he promote me in his love
To seat of grace, when my deliverance came.
From out the sea of gloom—

Enter ALDERMAN.

Alderman. Hail! pale-face,
And in thy wigwam peace!
    Church. Who art thou?
    Alderman. One that the wing of injury
Wafts to thy side.
    Church. Wampanoag?
    Alderman. Until to-day;
But while Pometacom folds him in flesh,
A hater of the name.
    Church. What wouldst thou do?
    Alderman. What ye have not yet done, though
      at your side
Cohorts of soldiers stood, and terror ran
Before your steps—I mean, if ye will not
Shudder, trap the fox of Pokanoket.
    Church. How shall we know
Thy words are clothed in true sincerity?
    Alderman. Test me by any proof thou wilt.
The unequalled genius of Pometacom
Was honored in my mind; I cut his wrongs
In stone of my devotion. Where he led
I followed, feeding the anger of my blood
With ruin of the whites. Close at my side
Fought Agamaug, my brother, in whose life
I ever spread the blanket of my love.
When turned the tide of fortune to the whites,
And our affairs that erst had rode in state

Now trudged afoot, my brother counselled peace.
For this offence he slew him; in his heart
Buried an inch of steel that split mine too;
And with that hand of wrong
Gouged out the eye of my esteem.
I am familiar with his plans, will lead
Thy forces to his hiding-place, and ask
No recompense: his fall will pay me all.
Still dost thou doubt? Guard me—place at my
 back
Spies to transcribe in volume of thy fear
Each look and word and act, till thou admit
The stars sooner will wander from their path
Than I from my revenge. See!

[*Takes a burning brand from the fire, and thrusts it in his arm.*]

If in the caverns of my blood there lurks
Merely a globule of respect for him,
I smoke it out.
   Church.   Enough! I do believe
Thine honesty pants at the very side
Of thy wild words. I will hear more of this.
Walk there aside.—Golding, double the guards.
If this be but a ruse, it takes us not.
As to the matter of our former speech,
If I have stepped out of my whilom self,
My change hath reason in it. But no more.
The morrow steals apace when we shall need
Our all of man to meet and push aside
That desperate arm. To rest awhile.—
Wampanoag!
   Golding. Our fortunes walk with thee!
[*Exeunt.*

SCENE V.—POKANOKET. A swamp. Remains of an Indian camp under the larch and spruce. The morning twilight.

Enter TUSPAQUIN *and* TATOSON.

Tuspaquin. Tatoson,
Vainly I seek in battle's crimson bed
Those shadowy arms: from my embrace they fly
Aghast, and leave me still alone with grief.
 Tatoson. Let not these inward fiends
Assail thee, Assawomset: time will smooth
His face to welcome, and in war's dread court
Divorce thy soul from this much-hated life.
 Tuspaquin. If he with torture or with banishment,
A heavier lot, had paid my grievous fault,
I would have smiled; but when I never hear
The foot of menace tread upon his lips,
Nor while his face sinks in that gulf of gloom
Speaking more loud than words his agony,
His looks and manners throw on me no blame,
I breathe but bear no life. In Pauguk stream
I will wash off the knowledge of myself. [*Exit.*
 Tatoson. If self-destruction mangled not
The body of our creed, he would conspire
'Gainst his own life.

Enter PHILIP *and* ANNAWAN.

Philip. Go at once
Unto the red oak swale: hence send a brave
To spy me if the whites have broken camp.
Bring me word here. [*Exit Tatoson.*
 Annawan,

We are a prey to fate, and in the throes
Of cold mortality our fortunes lie.
    Annawan.   Shake off those thoughts! If they
        still haunt thy mind,
Fling at them slaughtered men.
    Philip.   'Tis written on the sky!
The sun's red face was muffled in eclipse;
And on the silver arm of the wan moon
There hung a red man's scalp. The Manitou
Sorely is vexed, and turns his face away.
    Annawan.   Tush!
At the great bar he cannot charge that we
Folded the arms of duty, and let run
Unchecked this new disease in our dear land.
    Philip.   Bravest of men! how like a second self
Have been thy ways to me!
    Annawan.   Say not, Pometacom!
I love a battle better than a feast.
    Philip.   How many moons have brooched with
        light
The livid breast of night, since we began?
    Annawan.   Twelve as I think, Pometacom.
    Philip.   Thou art a novice in arithmetic:
In only twelve could treason spawn and hatch
Some monstrous brood? Say rather since the
        world
Wore infant looks, this hath been plotting. No!
We wage a war with phantoms of the air:
But strike them down, and feed the greedy earth
With what they have of blood, new forces rise
In mocking tongues to question our report,
And all our work undo.

Annawan.   Hath their great sea
Crumbled thy fortitude?
    Philip.   If in my veins a drop of blood
Courses that doth advise this heart to fear,
I beg thee sluice it out.
    Annawan.   My Sachem!
    Philip.   No!
I am a brother to the elements,
All iron as they are:
I would not make a sinner of my thoughts,
And clothe my latter days in infamy,
By bating but a jot the righteous hate
I bear that race.
              Re-enter TATOSON.

    Tatoson. The pale-faces have pierced the swamp.
    Philip.   How near!
    Tatoson.   Two bow-shots off.
          [*Yells and warwhoops in the distance.*
    Philip.   Fain would I borrow now
Smiles from my happier days, to greet this news.
Come, Annawan, there are lives to have.
    Annawan.   Now thou art perfect.   [*Exeunt.*

     Enter CHURCH, ALDERMAN, *and soldiers.*

    Church. That way they fled. Be vigilant and
        firm.
It is a blessed hand and bathed in gold,
That brings the head of the Pokanoket.
    Alderman. The voice of Agamaug speaks from
        the grave
Louder than thine.   [*Reports of guns.*
    Church.   Ha! their muskets call. Away!
                                           [*Exeunt.*

SCENE VI.—ANOTHER PART OF THE SWAMP. Some fallen trees on one side; on the other, higher ground covered with rocks and cedars. The day dawns.

Enter PHILIP, TATOSON, *and braves.*

Philip. Your loyalty revives my plant of life.
Post some upon that mound : I will defend
This forward path. Ask no quarter—give none.

[TATOSON *and part of the braves clamber up to the high ground.*]

Enter ANNAWAN.

Annawan. The cowards, pah ! to run at the first blow !
Nushkah ! I'd rather drill these sticks and stones
In forms of war, than captain such base creatures.
Philip. It matters not : here will I take my stand.
Many have travelled to the spirit land
Bearing my passport on their brow ; and more
The grim sentinel of that silent shore
Shall challenge. So, farewell, my grizzled brave !
Thee have I loved as father, friend, and guide,
In whose clear soul my purpose could reside
As in its native home—a long farewell !
And for a time condemn thyself to dwell
Among the race of men. Nay, do not stay !
Live to report me in my little day :
How worshipped I the dear Wampanoag name,
And toiled to blazon it in deeds of fame
On old tradition's scroll ; and when it fell,

That fatal hour did strike mine own death knell.
Why dost thou stand?

Annawan. Because I smell a danger;
For if I knew a village of delight
Where peace did dwell, and here unbottomed ran
Rivers of blood, nothing could stir me hence.
My hatchet laughs, my knife in ecstasy
Leaps to my hand, and calls it shame of shame
To kennel but in blood.

Enter SOLDIERS.

First Soldier. Surrender, Philip!
Annawan. Do not jest with us. [*Shoots him.*
First Soldier. I felt
The spur of glory, and lie here. [*Dies.*

Enter TUSPAQUIN.

Second Soldier. He wears a head of gold
Which must be mine. [*Levels his gun at Philip.*
Tuspaquin. Thine is too mean a hand.
[*Strikes down his musket and buries a knife in his throat.*
Gleams anywhere a blade
Hungry for blood, let it drink mine.
Third Soldier. Here, brighten this for higher
work!
Tuspaquin. No, thou must go to smooth my way.
[*Dashes his tomahawk in his brain.*
Why is it so?
I ask thee not for immortality.
Fourth Soldier. Let me but try this edge on
thee. [*Stabs Tuspaquin.*

  Tuspaquin.   How thou hast whetted it!—
Sachem Pometacom—   [*Dies.*
  Philip.   Brave Tuspaquin!—
Pale-face, he waits for thee!
[*Tomahawks and scalps him: holds aloft the scalp-lock
  and utters the terrible warwhoop.*]
I live again! Let him that hates the sun
Look on my face.
  Fourth Soldier.   Hell hound!
In thine own sulphur burn! How dark it is!
               [*Dies.*
  Annawan.   How triumph doth caress our hand!
  Come on!
  Philip.   Their spirits light my way.
I chide mine arm that is so merciful.
But here are more.

Enter GOLDING, ALDERMAN, *and soldiers on the rocks
  above. They fight with* TATOSON *and his braves
  and drive them off.*

  Alderman.   Down, and take him!
  Philip.   Dog! dost thou crawl
Back to my sight, to be whipped hence?
  Alderman.   The foot,
The stealthy foot of vengeance never sleeps.
  Philip.   On thy crossed brow
Black shame shall ever sit.
  Alderman.   My brother's love
Shall wash it pure as snow.
  Philip.   Never!
Together ye shall swim in pitchy waves
That roll on black hell shore—and on thy front

Lettered in fire that word of infamy,
Traitor. But touch the banks, a cloven foot
Deeper shall push you in.
 Golding. No parley! Philip, throw down thine
  arms,
And to our justice yield.
 Philip.   Come, and take them.
 Golding. The red bullet shall knock at thy
  heart.   [*Fires.*
 Philip. It shall be welcome.
I care not when I go, so that it be
In hand with honor. Herald me!

[*Hurls a tomahawk which grazes the cheek of* AL-
DERMAN *and sinks in the breast of a soldier.*]

 Alderman. Thy flint was cold:
For mine it is reserved.   [*Fires.*
 Golding.   He falls!
 Alderman.   And by his fall,
Ye are raised up.

 Enter CHURCH *and soldiers with captives.*

 Philip.   Annawan,
Thy hand—so! I had hoped to make our land
A graced place where no forest voices should
Impeach our power; and where in all his walk
The sun should cast no shadow of a white.
But my dear plans were snared in treason's net,
And it is time Pometacom stepped down
Into the silence.
Oh treachery! what soil was in my life
That thou shouldst grow so profligate and rank!
            [*Dies.*

Annawan.   My Sachem, art thou gone ?—
Pluck every fear out of your craven hearts ;
For he your dark despair in wonder robed,
Hath passed into his father's summer land.
　　Alderman.   My brother's ghost mourning be-
　　　　neath the clay,
Now, well-contented, travels on its way.
　　Church.   Thy deed speaks for thee, Alderman,
　　　　in tongue
Whose echo shall be heard around the world.
The ruined fields, the towns in ashes laid,
The sacred lives plunged in their timeless graves,
Gather to them a voice out of the dust,
And call thee to the banquet of their praise.
Misfortune dogs us all : I have a loss
Espousing me to sorrow through my life.
The path of satisfaction shalt thou tread ;
But I will house me by my noble dead,
Tokens to strew on that pathetic mound
Whose heaving turf my haggard thoughts will
　　　bound
Till death shall wave his banner on my brow.
Golding shall stamp the embers out ; but thou
Bequeath to me the arm that owes his life,
And on our borders quenched the fires of strife.
　　Alderman.   It is thine.

THE END.

www.ingramcontent.com/pod-product-compliance
Lightning Source LLC
Chambersburg PA
CBHW020101170426
43199CB00009B/359